The Lord Is My Shepherd–
Why Do I Still Want?

Rabbi Paul Plotkin

SUNBELT EAKIN  Austin, Texas

FIRST EDITION
Copyright © 2003
By Paul Plotkin
Published in the U.S.A.
By Sunbelt Eakin Press
A Division of Sunbelt Media, Inc.
P.O. Drawer 90159
Austin, Texas 78709-0159
email: sales@eakinpress.com
website: www.eakinpress.com
ALL RIGHTS RESERVED.
1 2 3 4 5 6 7 8 9
1-57168-754-8

Library of Congress Cataloging-in-Publication Data
Plotkin, Paul, 1950–
    The Lord is my shepherd : why do I still want? / Paul Plotkin.– 1st ed.
      p.   cm.
    Includes index.
    ISBN 1-57168-754-8
    1. Suffering–Biblical teaching. 2. Bible. O.T. Psalms–Criticism, in-
terpretation, etc. 3. Consolation. 4. Plotkin, Paul, 1950– I. Title
BS1430.6.S8 P56 2002
296.7'2–dc21   2002152660

This book is dedicated to Bubie Bella,
who always had the faith.

Contents

Introduction

Summer had always been my favorite time of the year. Traveling, time off work, and especially the time up at the lake in Canada . . . but not that summer. My wife of twenty-three years decided she was unhappy with our lifestyle and wanted out of the marriage. I was in a state of shock. My life as I had known it was over. All the shared dreams, all the plans, all of my basic assumptions were shattered.

I had just returned from leading a tour of Israel. No one on the tour had known exactly what was wrong, only that the Rabbi's wife had at the last minute been detained by work and could not come. No one knew that at the end of each day's excursion, I would cry myself to sleep. I was all alone in my deluxe, yet very empty suite.

To make matters worse, I was scheduled to spend the week after the tour with another couple, in Paris. The location was a choice my wife had made, and which I begrudgingly went along with. Now I was with them, but alone, in a city that was chosen for her pleasure. The sense of aloneness, the pain of the changes, the irony of the locale were more than I could bear. Yet my friends had planned the trip with us and were looking forward to that part of the vacation. They had been taken into my confidence regarding the family crisis, but insisted that I come with them. I kept up as strong a front as possible, while I continued to cry like a baby each evening.

On my second day in Paris, my first time on the Metro—indeed at the very first station—I felt a tightness on my body centered around my jeans pocket. I reached down for my wallet and discovered it was gone. I had been pickpocketed. My money, my documents, my credit cards and license were all gone. If there was palpable sadness before, and an overwhelming sense of vulnerability, there was now the sense of having been personally violated, as well. I could not wait to get out of France. I arranged for the first flight out.

That first week back I was informed that my wife would call and ask that we go public with the separation so that "she could go on with her life." I resisted. In fact, I was in denial that it could really happen. We had agreed to keep things under wraps for the summer while we pursued therapy and time apart. But the call came through as I had been told it would.

Later, alone at the cottage, the ancestral retreat that had all my life been my refuge and sanctuary, I was left to contemplate the shambles of my once successful and accomplished life.

I was mired in self-pity. *How could this have happened to me?* I wondered. Other people got divorced—not me. My life would be hell. I would never love or be loved again. My professional life would be compromised.

Who would want a divorced Rabbi? I thought. *What will happen to the kids? How will I be able to afford their education?*

There was no limit my mind's creativity at manufacturing fears. I didn't eat. I barely slept, and I was filled with nervous energy and a constant sense of pain and fear. The pain was so real, I could point to its exact location on the front of my chest wall.

In this angst, and with increasing fears, I got up one morning to begin my daily prayers. I donned my prayer shawl and phylacteries and began to pray as I had been doing every day for the thirty-one years since my Bar Mitzvah, only now I had a special message for myself.

"Okay, Paul " I said. "It's put-up-or-shut-up time. All these years, you've preached of the power of prayer. You've talked of how people in crisis could reach out to God for solace and strength. Now it is your turn. No one should feel alone if they believe."

If there was a listening and compassionate God, if He was, as Rabbi Harold Kushner had taught, the source of strength to get you through the crisis, then now was the time to call on Him.

Go daven *(pray) as you always did, only this time see if it can help,* I told myself.

I had thrown down the gauntlet—would I be helped?

I began the morning prayers, the same prayers I had said faithfully and regularly for more than three decades. The words were the same, but the speaker was altogether new. It didn't take long.

A few pages into the service, I began Psalm 30.

I extol you O Lord, for You have lifted me up . . .

The words got my attention.

Lifted me up.

I certainly could have used some lifting from the valley of my despair.

O Lord my God I cried out to You and You healed me.

I was crying out—would He heal me?

O Lord, You brought me up from the depths, preserved me from going down into the pit.

The psalmist was speaking to me; no, he was speaking *for* me. He understood, he'd stood at the edge of the pit, he knew the fear of falling in. We were kindred souls. He understood me as no one else. What would he say next, how did he handle it, I wondered. And then came the line that changed me:

At night one goes to sleep crying; in the morning there is the ringing cry of joy.

There was an immediate change in my mood. A weight was suddenly lifted, a heaviness that I had lived with for days was gone. I could feel the lightness. Like a banging headache that lingers to the point where you feel you will suffer with it forever. Now it was suddenly gone, leaving a real feeling of quiet and physical peace. For the next few minutes, I felt better. The cloud had lifted. Mysteriously, I no longer felt alone or helpless or doomed. Sunshine had entered and was illuminating me from the inside. In a split second, I had received an answer. There would be a future. I'd get through this. I got a pen and underlined the sentence.

In the days and weeks ahead, when the blues would strike, when the melancholy, fears, and uncertainties reemerged, I would return to that one line and regroup. I would again lose the negativity, regain a positive focus, and stabilize myself for the events that life had in store for me.

If the story ended there, this book would probably never have been written, but another surprise was waiting for me.

I was with a colleague on a long drive. We were recounting our summer experiences. Mine, which I just related, were by now very public and well known. His were a lot more private. He had been going through a lot of changes, as well, and he was searching for a way to cope. He told me that in addition to his daily prayers, he had begun to meditate. He took it very seriously and felt its benefits. His form of meditation required focusing on a statement. Being a Rabbi, he felt he should find a Biblical verse to meditate on. He searched all around for a verse that would resonate with a sense of calm. A verse that would speak to him in such a way that he could draw positive energy from it.

Curiously, I asked what verse it could be. Imagine my shock and surprise when, from all the wonderful and powerful verses in the Bible, he quoted the Book of Psalms, my chapter, my verse. I was shaking in excitement.

"When we stop, I want to show you something," I said.

At our next stop, I opened the trunk of the car, took out my Talis and Tephilin bag, removed my prayer book, and opened it to Psalm 30.

"Look at it," I said, "and notice what is underlined."

He and I had discovered the same line in the same psalm, as a comforting message to our personal pain. It was then that I knew I had to share the power of the Book of Psalms with everyone.

Psalms has a long history, in both Judaism and Christianity, as being the source of our liturgy. Perhaps it is because, unlike the rest of the Bible, in which God speaks to man, Psalms is a book in which man speaks to God. The psalmist, be he King David or be she some gifted poet, is in the end a human being, who underwent some life experience and wrote about it. They are like you or me, but they were blessed with the sensitivity of soul, and the talent of pen, to articulate their experience. We will see later that whether it was recovery from illness or loss, or dealing with fear or depression, they came through the experience and left us a summary of their soul's experience. When we read a psalm, we benefit from their experience. We hear their pain, feel their solace, and gain their strength and faith in the face of suffering and loss.

It is my intent to capture the voice of the psalmists. I want to further articulate their feeling and apply it to our circumstances today, by sharing a story that reflects what the psalmist is saying. If the reader can pick up any chapter in this book, read the verse(s) I have chosen, and then use my explanation or story to find the comfort I found in Psalm 30, then my work will truly have been, for me, a blessing.

— CHAPTER 1 —

Power of Prayer

*May the words of my mouth
and the prayer of my heart
be acceptable to You,
O Lord, my rock and my redeemer.*

(Ps. 19:15)

"If God is so wonderful, so powerful, so almighty, what does He need my praise for?" So begins a typical discussion that people have with me on the subject of prayer. They open a prayer book or a hymnal, they read a list of praises and adulation, and wonder what the point is.

Some assume it's like a cosmic "buttering up." If you praise God enough, you'll get Him in a good mood, and then you can sneak in the request.

It's like the teenager who tells his parents how well he's done in school, how popular he is with his peers, how proficient he is in athletics, and then says, "So you'll understand and not get angry when I tell you about how I smashed up the car last night."

Some think prayer is really magic, nothing more than an incantation. It's mumbo jumbo, they think. That's why Hebrew and Latin worked so well. And if the prayer is said in the prescribed manner and with all the correct rituals, God will be compelled into granting their request. Such a "religious" worshiper, when their prayer is not "answered," assumes it's because they did not pray correctly. The casual, uncommitted worshiper becomes angry with God for not listening to their prayer and says, in essence, "To hell with God if He can't be there for me when I pray." Different responses, but the same faulty premise. These two attitudes, and many other variants, all begin from the assumption that prayer was intended for God. After all, look to whom it is addressed. If I talk to you and call you by name, it's not a big stretch to say it's pointed in your direction. But is it really?

There are different kinds of prayer, to be sure. There is prayer of thanksgiving. The kind we're all familiar with.

"Thank you God for this beautiful meal we are about to partake in." Or the classic that is uttered spontaneously when the doctor comes in with the biopsy report and tells you it was benign: "Thank God." There are prayers of praise. We've all felt it and sometimes expressed it.

At a glorious sunrise at Ayers Rock in Australia, at a sunset on Mallory Pier in Key West, on a flyover at the Grand Canyon, we are so overwhelmed by the beauty of nature, so in awe of its creator, that we articulate an "Oh, wow" to the master of creation. Maybe it's the moment of birth of a child, the marriage of a daughter, or that classic television commercial moment when it "just doesn't get any better than this." That's when you pause to thank God for the glory of life.

There are prayers of petition, which we all chant in times of need. "Dear God, don't let it be cancer," or "O Father in heaven, let me get this job; pass this test; let her say yes to my proposal of marriage." These are all real prayers, no less valid than the ones you find in your prescribed prayer book.

They serve a real and different purpose from what we previously discussed was the mistaken purpose of prayer. *Real prayer is not directed to God, but rather through God to us.* When we offer prayers of thanksgiving, we are teaching ourselves to appreciate. It is so easy to take for granted that which we have, that which we do.

Must we lose it, to suddenly appreciate what we had? A praying person has the chance every day to reflect on his or her good fortune. To not take health or wealth or a good marriage for granted. Does it not follow that if I appreciate what I have and value it while I have it, I will not only enjoy it more, but I will invariably take better care of it? If I thank God for my body, I raise my level of appreciation for this body and therefore take care of it and do not abuse it. When I ask God for something, I'm forced to think about my needs.

I prioritize what is really important to me. I don't go to God with a shopping list of every need.

I, by definition, think and sort and separate the chaff from the wheat, the mundane from the essential. The act of a petitionary prayer focuses me and my energy.

In times of crisis, we are so scattered, so overwrought with fear and anxiety that we don't know what to do first. We go off in so many different directions that we dissipate our strength. We rob ourselves of our best effort. A prayer of petition to God can focus us and help direct us to a more effective agenda of activity and resolution. Similarly, a prayer of praise to God is not for His glory but for our own. We praise God because it makes us feel important. We are elevated by the company that we keep. Spend a day dressed like a bum surrounded by derelicts. Spend a day dressed in a tuxedo surrounded by others at a formal affair. You are the same person, but being in one company elevates you, while the other brings you down.

Another, more subtle, way of understanding this is to think of two different conversations you may have had in the course of one day.

The first may have been with some friends who enjoyed gossiping about your mutual acquaintances. There were the inevitable putdowns, the barbed comments and sarcastic references.

Later that day you met with people who discussed their commitment to charity work, or sat around over coffee and discussed a new and thought-provoking novel or play.

In both cases you were the same person. In both cases you were involved in talking. Yet which conversation was spiritually uplifting, and which left you a little empty and low? To praise God is to put oneself in an environment of the lofty and the elevated. To praise God is to engage one's faculties in matters of the holy, the special, and to rise above the mundane, the common, the boorish, which are so much a part of modern living.

To praise God, therefore, benefits us through our encounter with God. Prayer must impact on us, on the flesh and blood, if it is to have any significance.

Yet can I honestly tell you that every time I opened a prayer book, or every time I chanted an utterance to God, I was moved or directly impacted? Hardly! Indeed, the majority of times, my prayer tends to be rote, and I sometimes wonder if the seemingly small return of prayer justifies the effort.

But I know that every prayer, and every prayer service, is either preparing me for, or has the potential for being, that moment when I will speak to myself more profoundly, and with more impact on my life, than I could have ever imagined.

I know this because it happened to me when I was sixteen years old.

It was the summer of 1966, at a resort town on Lake Simcoe in central Ontario. We'd had a summer home there since the late 1930s, when many of our immigrant grandparents had purchased a summer getaway north of Toronto. My contemporaries and I were now the third generation spending their summers there. It was not uncommon on a Saturday night for a hundred or more teenagers to gather at some location for a party or to just "hang out." Later in the evening, groups of friends, usually based on age (i.e. licensed drivers, or not), would take off for the next adventure.

One evening we were at someone's cottage on a very large lot. There were teenagers all over the place. Some were talking, the younger ones were horsing around, the older ones were trying their luck at picking someone up.

In one corner, there was a mixed-age group playing a game of "levitation." The game was played by a few people who surrounded a volunteer lying prone on his back.

While chanting, "He is alive, he is dead; he is alive, he is dead," and by merely putting two fingers of each hand below the body, the group could raise the stiff body of the volunteer into the air.

According to the game's rules, if the body rose, he was alive, but if it failed to move, he was dead. I walked over to observe the game.

The body that evening belonged to a friend of my sister, a young boy of thirteen named Paul W. He was blond, good-looking, and very popular. "He is alive, he is dead; he is alive, he is dead," they chanted over and over again.

He didn't move at all.

I became bored and hooked up with my friends, the older boys, one of whom not only had his license but had the use of the car. Life was good as we left to cruise away the night.

Later on, we were on the main street, which paralleled the lake but was never closer than 200 yards to it. A little after you passed my street, which was the last street in the town, the lake curved in, and the road seemingly came out to meet it.

There was a sharp turn left, while on the right side of the road there was an exposed lip of a little cliff. It dropped immediately some twenty feet to the lake. As we passed my street, we noticed a lot of commotion up ahead. There were police lights everywhere, a tow truck, and other emergency vehicles.

For a small town in summer, this was excitement. We stopped our car, parked on the side of the road, and joined the other spectators. The truck with the winch was just then pulling up a station wagon that had been flattened into a metallic pancake.

Obviously, there had been an accident. The car had not been able to hold the road at the curb. It had gone flying over, and the force of the crash into the lake had made the car two-dimensional. We asked about the people and were told that all had survived and been taken to hospital. After a while we got back into our car and continued with the evening's activities.

The next morning I was enjoying a deep and much-needed sleep when in some part of the dream state I became aware of the sound of feet. They were rapidly ascending the wooden stairs of my cottage on their way to the sunroom, where I tenaciously was holding on to my sleep. "Quick, wake up, Paul," a voice seemingly from a great beyond was saying to me. "Remember the accident last night? After the party, Paul W. was hitchhiking home and he got a lift in the car that went over. The driver and other passenger will be all right, but he was killed. All the kids are gathering down at the pier."

By now I was stone-cold awake. I quickly dressed and threw some water on my face. As I went flying out of the cottage, I began to chant the prayer that I always said upon getting up in the morning. Under normal conditions, an observant Jew on rising washes his fingertips and eyes and then says the modeh ani: "I thankfully acknowledge before Thee O everlasting King for having returned to me my soul. With great compassion is Your faithfulness."

You need to understand that I had spent my first few years of life with my parents in my grandparents' house. Then, every summer, my mother would move into my grandmother's cottage with her and the grandchildren.

My grandmother was a domineering battle-ax of a woman who ruled her roost with complete authority, and I, as the first-born grandson, was the crown prince. Needless to say, I loved her deeply and the relationship was totally reciprocated.

She had a profound influence on me, not the least of which was teaching me the "modeh ani" prayer.

But her tutelage did not stop with mere teaching.

I never got up on a morning when she was around, that she didn't ask me in Yiddish, "Did you say the modeh ani today?" It got to the point that in the morning, in a semicomatose state, I could hear her voice even if she wasn't there.

In short, I never missed saying the prayer.

Here I was, sixteen years old, and probably had been saying the prayer for twelve years and it had never meant more, or had any more impact on me, than brushing my teeth in the morning. It was regular, routinized, and seemingly irrelevant—until that morning. I bounded out of the cottage, and just as I opened the gate to leave the yard, I said the modeh ani and froze in my tracks.

I began to shake. I had goosebumps, and my whole body was overcome with something, and I didn't know what. All I knew was that I was overwhelmed and that I was not in control of my body or of myself.

And then it hit me with the full clarity of a cloudless sunny day. Paul W. had died and it could have been me! His name was Paul, my name was Paul. He was at the party, I was at the party.

He drove by the curve in the road, I drove by the same curve. He didn't make it. I did. Paul W. was dead. Paul Plotkin was alive.

Modeh ani, Thank you God for giving me back my soul . . .

It was my first "religious experience." It was the first time I had a profound feeling, a message, a lesson, that I would never have had or never experienced at that level had it not been for that prayer.

For twelve years I said that prayer and received no obvious return.

Now I had this overwhelming sense of appreciation. Was it worth saying all that time for just that one experience? Absolutely!

I learned then that there were experiences, insights and awareness, that come to you in life, but only if you are open or prepared for them.

Lots of kids made it to the pier that day, and lots of kids shared feelings, but no one had the experience I had.

We all talked cognitively of a new appreciation of life, but I felt it in a way and in a place that none of my peers did or could.

That is why I pray every day, not only the modeh ani, which still holds a special power for me, but my other regular prayers, as well. You see, I want to be in shape. I want to be ready to receive the next special experience, whenever that moment will be. I don't know when or where it will happen, but if I continue to pray and keep those praying muscles conditioned, then when the opportunity arises, I'll be ready.

May the words of my mouth
and the prayer of my heart
be acceptable to You,
O Lord, my rock and my redeemer.

— CHAPTER 2 —

Abandonment

While I was on sabbatical in Australia, a friend and congregant lost her mother. When I found out, I e-mailed her my condolences and reached out as best I could from down under. After her mourning period, she sent me a long letter thanking me for my concern and taking me up on my offer for lunch on my return. She told me about her mom, and of the great loss, and then she said, "The reality of it hits me in spurts. I still can't believe she is gone. We now have no parents, which is the hardest thing of all. I can't tell people enough how important family is, that they are the foundation of your life and will always be there for you."

But what if they're not ? What happens if the time you most need them, they purposely abandon you? Can it get much worse than that? That is part of what the psalmist experienced in the lowest part of his life.

In Psalm 38 he cries of a life of misery, suffering, and pain. From God he has received punishment:

for Your arrows were fired into me, and down upon me has Your hand come . . . (vs. 3)

He recognizes his own responsibility in all this.

For my iniquities have gone over my head,
as an onerous burden;
they are too heavy for me . . . (vs. 5)

Society is out to get him with an attack of slander and lies, rumors and gossip.

They laid snares for me,
those who seek my soul
and those who seek my hurt
speak of destruction,
and upon deceits all day do they meditate. (vs. 13)

With all this he has a serious disease, a plague of some kind, possibly leprosy. The only hope for support he might have had were friends and family. Instead:

My friends and my companions
stand aloof away from my affliction;
my own family stand off at a far distance. (vs. 12)

Is there nothing more pathetic or more painful in this whole litany of problems than the abandonment by friends and family? We know that there are people who will be jealous of us, competitors in many venues who will not like us.

We know that misfortune can strike at any time, and that disease and illness are everywhere. Yet somehow it is reassuring to know that in the worst times, a loving family and one's close and dear friends will be there for us in a nonjudgmental way. Isn't that the essence of the saying "a friend in need is a friend indeed" or "blood is thicker than water"? You know that no matter what you've done, your family will be a source of strength and support for you.

Yet this is precisely what the psalmist does not get. Indeed, the absence of this love and support is seen as an equal part of the suffering. It equals disease, enemy slander, and Divine wrath. This description is not just some hypothetical case that may or may not have happened some thousands of years ago. This is ripped straight from the hearts and lives of thousands of people with AIDS. For at least the last decade, AIDS patients have had to live with a plague of "Biblical proportions." Right-wing moralists have pronounced this disease to be the punishment of God. People, strangers, have gossiped and speculated on how the disease was first acquired. Many AIDS patients have felt great guilt for their lifestyle, or for a one-time dalliance. And worst of all, friends and family were often uncaring or scared, embarrassed, unsupportive, or all of the above. What would frighten you more than that combination?

I was called one day to officiate at the funeral of a young man who had died in his early thirties. I entered the family room at the funeral home. The bereaved parents were in the room with their one surviving son. The parents were retired civil servants from Brooklyn, living in a homogeneous retirement development. One had the impression that entire blocks of Brooklyn apartment houses emptied out one day and immediately recreated themselves in rows of catwalk apartments in the southern tropics of Florida. Outside were many of the parents' friends, some who had been neighbors and friends for all the years up north. They had watched the deceased grow up and were now gathering for the service. I asked about the deceased's life and gathered as much information as I could.

He was single, never married, lived up north, and been brought back to Florida by his parents in the last stages of his illness. Here they could take care of him. He died at home in their apartment.

Toward the end of the interview, and feeling that I was missing something, I naively asked what he died from. The mother jumped in immediately in a loud and assertive manner. "Cancer," she affirmed.

"Mom!!!" her son intoned, half-question, half-statement.

"It was cancer at the end, you know, that's all he has to know or say."

In those days I may have been a bit slow, but I wasn't moribund. I finally figured it out. Their son had died of AIDS. They were embarrassed and used cancer as an acceptable smokescreen. I accepted the cancer diagnosis and sent the parents to the family room to meet with their friends. I asked their other son to remain behind.

I explained to him that this was his parents' home turf. Neither his late brother nor he were from here. Indeed, the brother lived on the other coast, in San Francisco. He would leave in a few days, yet his parents would stay on here in their community with their friends, and we were duty-bound to obey their wishes. He quietly acknowledged my argument and rejoined his parents.

After the funeral, as everyone was returning to their cars, the surviving son approached me, and I could see that he wanted to talk.

"My brother was gay and died of AIDS. My parents brought him down here so they could take care of him. I'm gay, and I'm dying of AIDS, as well. I wanted my brother's funeral to be a statement, but I see now that you were right. My agenda is not my parents', and they have to live here. When I die, it will be in San Francisco with my friends and community. It will be open and supportive, the way I want it to be. You were right for me not to put my agenda here first. This is my parents' community, and I need to respect that."

Despite his words, I went back to the office devastated. What hell had we piled onto this poor family? The first son had no community to help him, and so returned to parents who would stand by him—but only to an extent. The fear of what the neighbors would say turned the dying, and then the funeral service, into an ongoing sham. The son died under a lie. The parents grieved through the veil of a lie. The other brother had to swallow his true beliefs and then help perpetuate a conspiracy of silence that he was otherwise dedicated to ending.

Disease and death are hard enough to bear. We shouldn't complicate the suffering and add to the pain with judgmental values and abandonment behavior.

The psalmist in Psalm 88, verse 9, shows again how devastating is the loss of our friendship circles.

You have estranged my friends from me,
You have made me an abomination to them;
I am imprisoned and cannot go out . . .

He goes on again to make the point in verse 19,

You have estranged from me,
friend and companion,
from my acquaintances,
I am abandoned in darkness.

The response to suffering, disease, and misfortune must not be to add to the misery. We must support, love, and help the afflicted. If we were there to party with them in the past, we need to be there to cry with them, hug them, and support them in the present. Let God be the judge of people's behavior. Let us be the bearers of comfort, solace, and love.

— CHAPTER 3 —

Suffering

Suffering and religion seemed doomed to be forever intertwined. It is certainly true that many have come to religion from their sense of despair and painful affliction. It is as the dying Violetta in *La Traviata* sings: "religion is such a comfort to those who are suffering." Yet it is equally true that suffering and pain have sent millions fleeing from any belief in a superior being or a planned and just universe.

The question of how a just and caring God could create a world filled with pain and suffering, of trials for the righteous and jubilation for the wicked, has been with us from the very beginning. Every religion, indeed any philosophy that calls for anything short of random existence, must deal with this issue. The Jewish tradition puts the question in the mouth of Moses who asks of God, "Why do the righteous suffer and the wicked prosper?"

Psalm 73 is a record of one person grappling with this classic dilemma and his or her extraordinary solution to the problem. As we shall now see, the author went through the usual questioning, the subsequent doubts, and then something happened to change him forever. He begins by telling us the party line.

God is good to Israel, to those whose heart is pure. (vs. 1)

But from early on he had trouble "buying it." He saw too much of the corruption and of the success of the wicked.

> *As for me, my feet had almost strayed;*
> *my steps were nearly led off course,*
> *for I envied the wanton;*
> *I saw the wicked at ease.*
> *Death has no pangs for them;*
> *their bodies are healthy . . .* (vs. 2-4)
> *They scoff and plan evil;*
> *from their eminence they plan wrongdoing.*
> *They set their mouths against heaven,*
> *and their tongues range over the earth.*
> *So they pound His people again and again . . .* (vs. 8-10)
> *Such are the wicked;*
> *ever tranquil, they amass wealth.* (vs. 12)

He begins to wonder what the point of being good is. Why live life on the good and narrow, to willingly do without the ill-gotten gains, only to see the wicked luxuriate through life, while he suffers evermore?

> *It was for nothing that I kept my heart pure*
> *and washed my hands in innocence,*
> *seeing that I have been constantly afflicted,*
> *that each morning brings new punishments . . .* (vs. 13-14)
> *So I applied myself to understand this,*
> *but it seemed a hopeless task.* (vs. 16)

Clearly, he is about to give up and maybe go over to the "dark side," but something happened!

> *Till I entered God's sanctuaries*
> *and I understood what would be their end.* (vs. 17)

It all changed for him. He saw something, his eyes were opened, he had a new perspective, and suddenly life made sense. Balance was restored. Justice ruled supreme.

Only in slippery places do you set them down,
You hurl them down to desolation.
How suddenly are they ruined,
wholly swept away by terrors . . . (vs. 18-19)

Those who keep far from You perish;
You annihilate all who are untrue to You . . . (vs. 27)

What did he now know that he did not know before? What happened to him when he entered God's sanctuaries that affected him so?

Perhaps he was shown a different perspective, a different way of looking at life. Perhaps in the solitude and holiness of the temple area, he was able to distance himself from the struggle and the mundane, and see the world in a new way. Perhaps now he understood that life as we see it is really an illusion. That life is really played out over a much larger stage than we ever imagined or can even grasp. That life is acted on the stage of time, and what we think was an entire play is merely an opening act. Life's inequity, therefore, was only an appearance, caused by a time distortion built into our finite existence. If we were only given a time perspective, we would see justice prevail. If we could only view life through a multigenerational telescope, we would see it all play out in a favorable and just way. Perhaps that's what he saw in the sanctuaries and so was able to say,

Those who keep far from You perish;
You annihilate all who are untrue to You.

In Psalm 92 we see the same awareness yet again.

Though the wicked sprout like grass,
though all evildoers blossom,
it is only that they may be destroyed forever. (vs. 8)

There *is* justice in life, but our personal part in the drama is rather small.

Imagine a decent Russian citizen, a resident of Moscow during the Stalin days. He was deprived of his liberties, living under the tyrannical control of the KGB, unable to practice his religion or express his opinions. Perhaps he risks everything to keep a diary. He poses over and over the question of his existence and wonders why this is happening. Over the years, his physical deprivation is exceeded only by the mental cruelty of his society, and he continues to ask why. He dies, never having an answer or a hope that there will be a resolution.

Imagine his grandchild, in the late 1990s, finding his diary and being able to fill in a more favorable description of life in Russia. He despaired of ever seeing such a state. Imagine how much more endurable his life would have been if he knew he had to hang in and bear it, but that his grandchild would have a life of freedom and opportunity. His angst over the inequity of life might have well dissipated if he had seen the whole picture.

Every spring, the Jewish people gather around the Seder table to celebrate Passover, the festival of freedom. They remember how their ancestors were slaves to Pharaoh in Egypt, and how God saved them. He inflicted ten plagues on the Egyptians and drowned Pharaoh and his army in the Red Sea. They celebrate the holiday for its statement of liberation, the end of suffering, and punishment of the wicked. Yet how would a Jewish slave, one generation before Moses and the liberation, have felt about life and God? He, too, would have asked the eternal dilemma of his suffering and the Egyptian prosperity. Yet time has given that slave's ancestor an entirely different perspective.

Imagine a Jew in Auschwitz eventually led to the gas chamber. Each day he may well have asked the eternal question. Why was the Nazi guard laughing, living well, while he was starving on the path to extermination? Yet his surviving son's son, alive and practicing his Judaism in the 1990s, sees no Hitler and no Nazi state. He does see a flourishing Jewish state of Israel, a prosperous Jewish community around the world, and even a renewal of religious practice. Indeed, he would see the resurgence and rapid growth of the Hasidic community, the segment of the Jewish population most devastated by the Nazis, now experiencing exponential growth. The grandson would never think to raise the question, while the grandfather would have found in this scene from the future, the very answer to the question.

Yet I can't help wondering whether our psalmist didn't see something else in that moment of insight.

Till I entered God's sanctuaries
and I understood what would be their end. (vs. 17)

What is the significance of the fact that he refers to *sanctuaries* in the plural? Had this insight come to him on a pilgrimage to Jerusalem, it would have been singular. There is only one sanctuary in the holy city. Unless where he visited or what he saw had nothing to do with this world at all.

The medieval Jewish commentator Ibn Ezra opens up the thought that what the psalmist saw was not of this world but a glimpse into the existence of eternity. He was given a vision of the world to come. What if this real struggling and suffering person was somehow made to believe that this world is just the antechamber, the vestibule, the corridor to the real and infinite existence of the afterlife? If that was his experience, then certainly he now understood the dilemma and was freed from it.

Of what use is the accumulation of power and wealth if you can't take it with you? Success in this world is mere folly if in eternity you are punished for its unlawful accumulation. Who is really suffering when the righteous souls are sent to a wonderful afterlife and the souls of the wicked must suffer? Maybe that is what the psalmist alludes to in verses 24 and 25.

With Your counsel You will guide me,
and afterward, with Your glory You will receive me.
Whom have I in heaven [but You]
and besides You I desire nothing on earth.

This is a theme that is referred to in a number of psalms.

In Psalm 37 he starts by addressing the very angst we began with.

Do not be vexed by evil men;
do not be incensed by wrongdoers;
for they will soon wither like grass.
And as the green herb they will fade away . . . . (vs.1)

The Lord is concerned for the needs of the blameless;
their portion lasts forever *. . .* (vs. 18)
For the Lord loves what is right,
He does not abandon his faithful ones.
They are preserved forever,
while the children of the wicked will be cut off.
The righteous shall inherit the land,
and abide forever in it. (vs. 28-29)

Wouldn't such an awareness truly liberate us from the perpetual dilemma of the suffering of the righteous? Wouldn't such a belief restore hope, pleasantness, and joy to our lives?

But can we really believe in it? Despite the testimonies of Shirley MacLaine and the past-life regression therapies, has anyone really ever come back to tell us that it exists? I believe in an afterlife, based in large part in my work on the "chevra kaddisha," the Jewish Holy Burial Society. I believe it is possible to know of the existence of something that is invisible, by sensing its absence. This is best explained by using a balloon. Imagine in you mind's eye a small red balloon. It just came out of its bag, and you examine it before inflation. Is there a lot of air in it? The answer would be "no." Now inflate the balloon. Tie it off. Is there air in the balloon? "Yes." Can you see it? "No, but I know it's there, even though I can't see it because the balloon is inflated." Now release the air. Is there a lot of air in the balloon? "No." Was there ever air in the balloon? "Yes. Even though I never saw the air, I knew it existed by the fact that at times it was gone."

We can recognize the prior existence of something by the times it is absent. That has always been my experience when I observe or participate in a "Tahara," a ritual washing and preparing of a dead body for burial. I still remember the first time so vividly.

I was called at 11:00 one night in response to my request to observe a "Tahara." It was early in my career, and though I had preached the virtues of a traditional Jewish burial, I had never been privy to the actual work itself. So I requested to be an observer at the first convenient time. This was to be it.

I dressed quickly but with considerable trepidation, for I was about to come face to face with my first dead body.

I drove to the mortuary and was let in by one of the members of the chevrah. These were observant men (women have their own chevrah) who for no salary, but only in fulfillment of the religious commandment of giving a proper and dignified burial, were out this late night to perform the rituals on a complete stranger. The body was lying on a marble slab with only a small towel covering the genitals. The group, with an absolute minimum of talk and with great awe and respect, began the first step of washing, cleaning, and combing the body. Only when this was done were they ready for the ritual purification of the body in a pool of water. The facility had such a pool, and to immerse the body, they had a sliding hoist. A number of belts were placed under the body, which was then hoisted into the air and pulled along an overhead track until it was lowered into the pool. Then it was raised again, dried, dressed in special white linen garments, and finally put into the casket. All this was accompanied by verses from the Bible.

It was when they first lifted the body that I realized that something was totally different here. The human body is rounded. It has curves. If you were asleep with no clothes on and someone from the side saw you in bed, they would have seen your torso and noticed that though you lay flat on your back, the sides of your body were rounded. This body was not. It had compressed and flattened out in the hours since death. Moreover, the marble slab had a pattern cut into it. The entire back and buttocks of the deceased had now been formatted with that pattern. It was, in a gross and in a truly bizarre way, the same as a piece of meat that you purchase from the butcher. Meat which has sat on a Styrofoam pad for a while, when you open it from the package, has the Styrofoam pattern embedded in it. Only this was not a piece of meat, this was a man! Once a father, a grandfather, a husband. Now where was he?

Later I looked into his eyes and noticed the other dramatic change. When you look at a living person, even one in a coma, they have a light reflecting back at you. It actually looks like a little rectangle of light that glistens. When you die, the light in the eyes is gone. Worse yet, the eyes are like dark holes swallowing the light into a deep abyss. There is a haunting emptiness seen through the eyes. This person that day, as every living person, had something, an energy that is in us in life and was now missing in death.

Based on my earlier premise, I now know that it exists even though I never saw it, because I knew when it was missing. If as we all learned in basic science, energy cannot be created or destroyed, and there was energy in the body, where did it go?

I like to call that energy the soul, and I believe that it is of and from God. As such, it is infinite and eternal, as is God. It is put in the body at some point in our making, and it leaves when we die. Indeed, death can be defined as the moment the soul leaves the body. The soul then departs the limitations of the body and returns. To where?

That place is the World to Come, or the afterlife, or Heaven or Hell, or a different consciousness, the great spirit world, Valhalla . . . It doesn't matter what your tradition calls it. It matters only that you believe in it, because if you do, then all those questions of the inequality and lack of justice in life are now answered. What you see is not what you know to be, and what you know to be is not what you see.

Till I entered God's sanctuaries
and I understood what would be their end.

— CHAPTER 4 —

Appreciation

A true story (because why bother with fiction when real life is so bizarre?). I was called to officiate at the funeral of a ninety-year-old woman. As is often the case, the deceased and the family were unknown to me. We met for the first time a half-hour before the funeral in the clergy room. A tension in the air was inhibiting my interview. I needed to find out about the deceased's life in order to prepare the eulogy, and time was fleeting. I gazed about the room at the children, old enough to be the deceased in someone else's scenario, the grandchildren almost old enough to be grandparents themselves. If ever there was a family that had a right to say, "This is good, it was time," this was it. Yet that was exactly what was missing. The interference I was experiencing came from the fact that the children were angry. Angry at whom, I was not yet sure.

Had the doctors made a mistake? Had there been family neglect, now displaced as projected anger? I continued to probe, hoping to release the genie and open the way for some real information. I was not prepared for what I got.

They were angry at God. How could He have let her suffer so these last few months? The disease was horrific in its final stage, and the last three months had been particularly intolerable. How were they supposed to believe in a God who could let

Mom suffer so? And then came the startling comment that threw me for a loop: "She hadn't been sick a day in her life till this illness." Indeed, in her ninety years, except for childbirth, she had never been in the hospital.

I kept waiting for the *but,* the zinger, the reason for the anger. Then I realized that was it. That was the focus of the anger. Mom never suffered before, so why now?

I wanted to scream out at the top of my lungs, "Do any of you hear what you are saying? Do the words that leave your lips penetrate your ears? For eighty-nine and three-quarters years, she had relative good health, and for three months she suffered, and you are complaining? Where do I sign up for this 'punishment'? By my calculations she enjoyed 99.72 percent of her life in good health, and now you have a complaint to God, because the last .28 percent was painful?"

Later I remembered a part of a psalm that reminded me that it has always been thus, Psalm 30, verse 7:

When I was untroubled,
I thought, "I shall never be shaken."

When we're on top of the world, it's because *we* earned it. We deserve it. We made it happen. It was our intelligence, our diligence, our skill, our risk-taking that got us to the top. For almost ninety years, the family at the funeral took Mom's good health for granted, or assumed Mom was strong and lucky. Maybe she had good genes or took particularly good care of herself. The one thing I'm sure they never said was, "Thank God for the blessing of Mom's longevity and good health." Like the psalmist, when you're on top, *you* did it. When you fall, then it's God's fault. And to what gain? These angry people, did they receive any comfort at the funeral?

Mom's life was there for them to appreciate and to inspire hope for their own lives. They did, after all, share her genes. Might not the blessings of mom's longevity also be theirs as a blessing? They would not see that. They were blinded by the anger and the bitterness of the end. They were so stuck in their anger that they missed the chance for inspiration, hope, and even joy that appreciating God's gift of their mother's life could have given them. They had a choice to give thanks and praise and be soothed and comforted. They chose to be angry and accusatory, and all that did was grate on the nerves and discomfort them. The psalmist finally understood:

I called to you, O Lord;
to my Lord I made appeal . . . (vs. 9)
You turned my lament into dancing,
You undid my sackcloth and girded me with joy,
that my whole being might sing hymns to You endlessly;
O Lord my God, I will praise You forever. (vs. 12-13)

If this family had only been accepting of the blessing of their mother's life, then her passing could easily have been turned into a celebration, of the gift that was her life and the hope that it would continue for them.

CHAPTER 5

Let God In

How long, O Lord; will you ignore me forever?
How long will you hide your face from me?
How long will I have cares on my mind,
grief in my heart all day?
How long will my enemy have the upper hand?
Look at me, answer me, O Lord my God!
Restore the luster to my eyes,
lest I sleep the sleep of death;
lest my enemy say, "I have overcome him,"
my foes exult when I totter.
But I trust in your faithfulness.
My heart will exult in your deliverance.
I will sing to the Lord,
for He has been good to me. (Ps. 13, vs. 1-6)

We've all been there, haven't we? We read the first few sentences and we identify all too clearly with the anguish and the despair. Who hasn't felt sorry for themselves and wondered why it was happening to them?

"What did I do to deserve this?

How long is this pain and suffering going to continue?

Where are you, God? Why have you abandoned me?

I don't know how much more of this I can take!"

The psalmist's language may be more flowery, but the pain is all too familiar to us. Even the rather clear reference to suicide (lest I sleep the sleep of death) is familiar to anyone whose felt that empty sense of helplessness. Maybe better to end it all in one quick moment than to experience the slow draining of my life's energy.

Why wake up every day knowing that each day will be worse than the next? Why watch as others take advantage of me, exploit me, while I am helpless to change anything? Slowly, the "luster of my eyes" diminishes until I am a hollowed-out remnant of myself, racked with the pain of failure and the emptiness of having no way out. Better to end it now!

Yet the same person who wrote the beginning of the psalm ended up "singing to the Lord."

What happened in the space of the few verses that changed his or her life? How can someone go from suicidal musings to jubilant singing and praise? What is the fulcrum of change in the psalmist's life that allowed for the almost miraculous, life-altering change?

The answer is actually rather simple and situated appropriately in the center of the psalm. The person suffering so greatly prayed to God.

Look at me, answer me, O Lord my God!

Nothing fancy, no great poetic breakthrough, just the most basic and sincere form of prayer possible. It was a heartfelt cry for help from a person in pain.

Did God answer? We don't know. The person records no change in the externals of their life, yet he went from the sadness of despair to the joy of song, through the one act of calling out.

He took control of his life. His despair came out of a sense of helplessness. Everything wrong in his life was external. God abandoned him. His enemies had the upper hand. In his mind he was always the victim, yet it was in his giving control to the powers without that the seeds of his pain and suffering were sown.

As long as his situation was caused by others, as long as he saw himself as a powerless victim, he had no response other than the sadness that comes from a state of hopelessness. His redemption came only when he internalized control of his life. When he *did* something. And the something he did was to call out and to pray.

Now he was empowered. He had a course of action that empowered him to do something. He didn't just sit as a passive victim who had to "take it." With the cry to God, our sufferer shirked the mantle of a helpless victim. He took back control of his life. For prayer is the power of the poor and the oppressed.

The mighty, the rich, the powerful, and the corrupt may control society. They may affect our options for employment and acquisition of material gains, but only we can abdicate to them control of ourselves.

When we pray and are certain of a listening ear, then we are somebody. We have status and rank and *we* control it. We can never again feel that helpless, or that alone. If we can pray, then we are empowered; and the *act* of prayer, not the *result,* is the source of that liberating power.

A Jew might have been victimized by the Nazis as he was taken for slaughter to the gas chamber, but the prayer that was said on the way ennobled him with dignity and empowered him to escape the feeling of being nothing more than a sheep to the slaughter. To be able to pray is to have control and ultimately power, for no matter what is done to you, you are still in charge of yourself.

Rabbi Bradley Shavit Artson tells about the power of prayer and the joy and comfort in learning to connect with Him.

> When I was a child, and throughout my high school years, I was a fervent atheist. I knew that the universe was a coincidence and that the emergence of human life was fortuitous. The evidence for my conviction was not hard to find; the extraordinary amount of suffering that all human beings endure, the tragic deaths of countless children to cancer or leukemia or sudden infant death syndrome, the disappointments of aging and of losing those we love, and the randomness of the way good people suffer and bad people prosper. All of these factors confirmed for me that life did not have any purpose; it simply happened.
>
> That being the belief of much of my family, I was quite comfortable with my atheism. I grew up assuming that "religious"

was a synonym for "dumb," and that religious people were simply cowards unwilling to face the universe and its indifferent reality. My mother's friends ignored religion except as a cultural artifact. Most of my playmates were also atheists—not out of conscious rebellion against the normal standard, but simply following in the footsteps of our families. Our free-thinking was a matter of habit.

While I (and my Jewish buddies) participated in becoming a Bar Mitzvah, it was only because of my father's adamant insistence. I accepted his explanation that he had become a Bar Mitzvah, and so had his father, and all of our male forebears since the beginning of the rite. From my perspective as a twelve- year-old, the fact that half of my ancestors had participated in what seemed to me to be a stifling and irrelevant performance was not a sufficient reason for me to waste my time. Besides, I hated services. From my twelve-year-old point of view, they were boring, hypocritical, and cold. I became a Bar Mitzvah simply because my father wanted it.

All of this seems noteworthy only in hindsight, from the perspective of a rabbi. From birth until college, however, I was a self-assured atheist.

Except for one brief interlude; when I was twelve, I began to suffer from a painful and embarrassing illness that produced oozing sores on the surface of my skin. This disease struck me in the midst of puberty and in the most private of places. I was so ashamed that I did not tell anyone for two years. I bled, suffered, and even cried in silence. Surrounded by loving people, I was still alone. Finally, in my first year of high school, when the pain was more than I could bear, I revealed my secret to my stepfather.

The next day, I was in the proctologist's office. He put me on an examination chair, face down, with my feet strapped into stirrups so he could explore without interruption. In my memory, the exam took hours. It was the most painful experience I can remember.

A few days later he told my mother of the pathologist's report: I had a terminal, inoperable cancer. The medical treatments for that illness (he turned out to be wrong about both its fatality and its inoperability) continued for more than ten years.

In that examination room, strapped to a chair, humiliated, and in great pain, I had an overwhelming experience of God. Devout atheist that I was (and would remain for several more years), one image kept flashing in my mind. All I could think of was Moses crossing the Red Sea—his courage in confronting Pharaoh, and his joy of liberation. I kept asking God to be with me and felt a strange comfort in the request, which I repeated over and over. God was with me in that room, in my pain.

Once the examination ended, I forgot about God and about Moses. Until recently, I never thought about it again. But I see it now as the beginning of the path that led me back to Judaism and, ultimately, to Jewish observance and celebration. In retrospect, that moment was the first time God broke through my barriers, no longer able to stand aside and wait. My pain was too much; God simply acted.

With further thought, I realize that God was there not only in my awareness of Him but in everything that was going on. God was in the hands of the doctor who was causing me so much pain in the process of trying to help, in the nurses standing by his side, and, most of all, in my mother, who nervously waited nearby. (Is there a better model of divine persistence and love than that of a parent who stays with her child through his pain?) In fact, there was nowhere that God was not present. And there never is.

But we do not know how to identify our encounters with God; we do not call them by their proper name. So pervasive is God's love and support that we do not notice it anymore The permanance and accessibility of miracles is the undoing of true religion; until we know our experiences for what they really are, until we can see God in the face of a child or the marvel of a new morning, we will always be indifferent to prayer.

The issue of prayer is the issue of God. Do we let God into our lives? Are we comfortable being uncomfortable in the presence of the Creator of the Universe? Do we dare pour out our hearts before God?

I will sing to the Lord,
for He has been good to me.

— CHAPTER 6 —

The "Coach" of My Team

My congregation has long ago gotten use to the fact that I make allusions to sports in many of my sermons and talks. In fact, I found out, after the fact, that a few years ago during the High Holy Days, there was a pool. People had bet on how long it would take before I made a sports reference in one of the many sermons and talks delivered during that most sacred of times.

One of my close friends had chosen an early number and was sure he'd win. He still has not entirely forgiven me for choosing that one year to be the time I made no sport references at all.

The truth is that in addition to being a sports fan, I see in sports many metaphors or lessons about the nature of real life. Maybe that's why we play and enjoy watching sports so much.

The most popular sport in the United States is football. Some say it is because of all the betting that takes place. That may be true, but for us true fans, there is so much emotion riding on our team that a bet would only be an unnecessary distraction. I think that pro football is so popular because it teaches us a special lesson on the meaning of redemption in life. Specifically, that there is failure and loss in life, which is not necessarily terminal. There is a chance to start over and a reason for hope, even in the direst of times.

Look at the rhythm of game week. We start on Monday with hope and anticipation. On the first Monday of the season, no one has yet lost, and all is possible. The hype begins as we talk of our strengths and our enemy's weaknesses. We speculate on what we and they will do and utter a silent prayer on behalf of our victory. We find all kinds of indicators that hint at our physical and spiritual superiority and argue for why it is right and just that we win. (How many times is loss seen as unjust: "If only we hadn't thrown that interception, we had them." Or my favorite, "The referee made a bad call that cost us the game.")

When we win, we experience a sense of joy and jubilation. We are elated with "our" victory. When we lose, there is a sense of great sadness. Later in the season, as the stakes rise, a loss has a sense of personal collapse and the sadness has escalated to a feeling of depression and anger. We often hear statements of abandonment, frustration, and despair.

"I give up on these guys; I've had it with these losers; I'm not going to or watching another game. It's too painful." And if the loss comes in the last seconds of a game that we thought we had well in hand, we get the anger mixed with medical concern, "My heart can't take another minute of this." (I actually have a friend who tapes all games and then his wife tells him if his team won or lost. If it is a win, he watches; if a loss, he skips the game. It seems that otherwise, to watch the game live, affects his blood pressure and is too threatening to his health.)

The promises of withholding our affection and concern prove to be short-lived. By Tuesday they start with new hype. There is a new challenge that we have to overcome. They'll find a new way to win. The coach comes on the air and tells us, as he has told the team, that there is reason to hope. They're still in the race for the wild card (or in the worst case, they're playing for jobs for next year, when they will definitely be playoff material). On any given day in the NFL, someone can beat everyone. A star player will be coming off of injured reserve and will be just the spark the team needs.

By Saturday we start believing all over again. We believe in the hope that springs anew from within. By Sunday, despite our earlier oaths, we attend the game or tune in on TV to watch, to cheer, and to hope that this week we'll get it right.

This will be the week we'll win and turn it all around. From this point on, our bad luck ends, the losing stops, and we will somehow make our goal. Being a true, dedicated fan of the NFL is just the same as living and believing in God's world. Ask the psalmist of Psalm 118. He feels the same way, only to him, the coach is called God.

> *The Lord is on my side;*
> *I have no fear;*
> *what can man do to me?*
> *With the Lord on my side as my helper,*
> *I will see the downfall of my foes.*
> *It is better to take refuge in the Lord*
> *than to trust in mortals;*
> *it is better to take refuge in the Lord*
> *than to trust in the great.* (vs. 6-9)

We can hear the life experience of the author of this psalm. He has already experienced his fair share of suffering. He has obviously had all kinds of run-ins with the people in his area. Some of them are his enemies, who are rather formidable. We assume by the beginning of the psalm that his enemies have had some measure of success. He probably trusted in people to help, and all that led to was failure and maybe betrayal. He could give up. We've seen that behavior in many. Instead, he realizes that the failures of yesterday count for little, because he has a second chance. He has a new coach to believe in, a chance for redemption from the failure of the past. He is euphoric. His confidence is at an all-time high.

"Enemies, bring them on, I have a new outlook and a new coach. Hit me with your best shot. I can take it and come out victorious."

> *All nations have beset me;*
> *by the name of the Lord I will surely cut them down.*
> *They beset me; they surround me;*
> *by the name of the Lord I will surely cut them down.* (vs. 10-11)
> *The Lord is my strength and might;*
> *He has become my deliverance. . .* (vs. 14)

Open the gates of victory for me
that I may enter them and praise the Lord.
This is the gateway to the Lord.
The victorious shall enter through it.
I praise You, for You have answered me
and have become my deliverance. (vs. 19-21)

I may have been on a lousy team in the past, one that everyone had given up on, but with my coach and his guidance and confidence I have succeeded. It's time to party—open up the champagne bottle.

The stone that the builders rejected
has become the chief cornerstone.
This is the Lord's doing;
it is marvelous in our sight.
This is the day that the Lord has made.
Let us exult and rejoice in it. (vs. 22-24)

In the game of life, when things don't go well, don't listen to the sportscaster, the sportswriter, or your football-maven neighbor. Trust in "Coach," who will show you a way. "Coach" will encourage you, guide you, and finally lead you through the "gates of victory." It's happened before and happens often enough. Upsets are a part of the world order. If you believe and stay loyal you will finally get to the promised land.

Speaking personally as a Dolphin fan, may that Super Day in January come yet again so that we can *"exult and rejoice in it."*

— CHAPTER 7 —

God Is Near

Applying to Rabbinical school was like running the gauntlet. After a year of preparation, preliminary interviews, essays, and study, I had to come to New York for the final run. For three days I was examined in Bible, Talmud, Hebrew, and more. Finally, with the test results in front of them, a panel of seven inquisitors began to ask me questions. They would eventually ask me very pointed questions about the essays I had written, especially about personal lifestyle issues, but first they softened me up with small talk.

Seeing as I was a Canadian, and there were two other expatriates on the committee, the subject began with hockey. I was lulled into a calm, not expecting the zinger that was coming later. By way of transition, they switched to a substantive but not yet personal question.

"How many times in the day," they wanted to know, "was Psalm 145 said in the Jewish Liturgy?"

On the surface the question seemed rather simple. It is said in the morning service and then again at the afternoon service. It is not said at the evening service, so it is easy to quickly respond, "Twice." It is easy, but wrong!

It's a trick question. The psalm is so important that it is repeated in the concluding portion of the morning service. It is in fact said three times.

I almost fell for the bait before I regained my mental composure and answered correctly. Ever since that interview, the psalm has had a special place in my consciousness.

It also obviously mattered to the editors of the Jewish prayer book. It is so powerful and important that I want to dedicate a number of chapters to elucidating only a part of its many messages.

I will extol You, my God and king,
*and bless Your **name** forever and ever.*
Every day I will bless You
*and praise Your **name** forever and ever.* (vs. 1-2)

The understanding of these verses, I owe to my children when they were little. By second grade, my children returned from school with a new vocabulary. Being in parochial school, it was not surprising that they were already speaking English and Hebrew. It was the third language, which they spoke in code to their friends, that was a little distressing.

The new language was profanity and obscenity. Mercifully, they already had enough upbringing to know that this language was unacceptable at home—thus the code. They would talk about the "f- word" or the "s-word," knowing full well what the words were, but exercising enough discipline or fear not to use the originals.

Later, on reflection, I realized that there was an irony in the way my children, their friends, and their friends' parents handled the new vocabulary.

These very words, which the kids and their friends were embarrassed or frightened to say, their parents tended to use rather freely. Yet there was one word that the kids had no difficulty saying but was virtually eliminated in the vocabulary of their parents. The word was known as the "g-word."

And "g" was God.

From nursery on, God, or the name my children called Him by, Hashem (lit. "the name") was something very close, very personal, and very real to them.

They talked to Hashem. They prayed to Him, blessed Him, and truly felt close to His presence. They would sing a song at school and at home when they went to bed. They would chant, "Hashem is here, Hashem is there, Hashem is truly everywhere." To their young and open minds, Hashem was a real force, a powerful force, an ever-present force. Most importantly, Hashem was a given, not a question.

To the parents of my children's generation, my contemporaries, Hashem had become a question, as in, "Do you believe in God?"

When they referred to Him, if at all, it was as God the deity, the distant force, or less. He was the "opiate for the masses," a construct for the weak and feeble-minded, or merely the universal equivalent of "to whom it may concern."

Adults did not talk about God except at tragedies, when it was time to blame Him for every suffering and every wrongdoing in the world. He didn't exist unless a scapegoat was needed or a whipping boy was desired by some victim. Most of the time, God was a leftover concept of our youth; nonrelevant and nonfunctional. A subject best left undiscussed.

In other words, ironically, God talk was taboo, treated in a similar way to obscenity. It was not used in public, or was spoken in code, using the "g-word."

The ability to speak God's name, to praise Him, is an expression of the closeness we feel.

The psalmist had no questions about God's existence. He lived with God as an ever-present partner in his life. He, like my children, had great joy and comfort in having someone so special and so powerful, so close to him in his life. That's why he begins with twice referring to "praising and blessing," because it's such a pleasure to be in close communication with God. He feels so close that he talks to Him by name:

I will extol You, my God and king
*and bless Your **name** forever and ever.*
Every day I will bless You
*and praise Your **name** forever and ever.*

— CHAPTER 8 —

Let Him In

Great is the Lord and much acclaimed;
His greatness cannot be fathomed.
One generation shall laud Your works to another
and declare Your mighty acts.
The glorious majesty of Your splendor
and Your wondrous acts will I recite.
Men shall talk of the might of Your awesome deeds,
and I will recount your greatness.
They shall celebrate Your abundant goodness
and sing joyously of Your greatness.
The Lord is gracious and compassionate,
slow to anger and abounding in kindness.
The Lord is good to all,
and His mercy is upon all His works.
And Your works shall praise You, O Lord.
And Your faithful ones shall bless You.
They shall speak of the majesty of Your kingship
and speak of Your might,
To make His mighty acts known among men
and the majestic glory of His kingship.
Your kingship is an eternal kingship;
Your dominion is for all generations.

The Lord supports all who stumble
and makes all who are bent stand straight.
The eyes of all look to You expectantly,
and You give them their food when it is due.
You give it openhandedly,
feeding every creature to its heart's content.
The Lord is beneficent in all His ways
and faithful in all His works.
The Lord is near to all who call Him,
to all who call Him with sincerity.
He fulfills the wishes of those who fear Him;
He hears their cry and delivers them.
The Lord watches over all who love Him,
but all the wicked He will destroy.
My mouth shall utter the praise of the Lord,
and all the creatures shall bless His holy name forever and ever.
     (Ps. 145, vs. 3-21)

The following is a true story that happened to me in my earlier years in the rabbinate. Its connection to this Psalm will become all too clear.

The telltale signs of the death watch were all around. I could sense it even as I walked along the catwalk of the condo, looking for the apartment.

I had received a call the day before from a member of the congregation. As a favor, would I visit one of his neighbors, a nonmember, whose wife was very ill and asking for a rabbi?

As I opened the door, I could sense the stillness that I had come to associate with these circumstances. The nurse's aide was sitting in the little kitchen, reading a newspaper to help pass the time during her eight-hour shift. The husband ran to the door to greet me in hushed tones. He wanted to prepare me, to explain what I already knew and had already sensed.

We walked into the bedroom, now a makeshift hospital room. There was the rented hospital bed, the oxygen tank in the background, and the patient, lying in the middle of the bed, a thin, emaciated shell of her former self. I had never met her before, but even from a skeleton, you can reconstruct a person in her prime. It was easy to see that she had once been an attractive and vibrant woman.

I stood at the bedside of this frail, seventy-three-year-old woman, not sure what I would say or, indeed, why I was there.

She quickly removed my uncertainty by looking at me and saying, "Rabbi, I want to feel God inside of me. Right now I feel nothing."

What did she want from me? What did she really expect? Was there a "God pill"? Was there an intravenous with God in it that I could put directly into her? What could I say to her? What could I do that would either meet her need or reduce my sense of inadequacy?

Immediately, I turned my professional cap around and went from rabbi to psychologist. What did she really want? More importantly, what was she really saying? What was she feeling? I had to find out where she was really coming from, and so I took a calculated risk.

"You feel angry, don't you?" I asked.

A spark ignited inside her eyes. I could see energy pulsating through her body.

Her head rose slightly, and she said, "Yes, I'm angry, Why me? Why is this happening to me? I've been a good person. This is not fair. Life's not fair, I don't deserve this."

I prodded. I led her in her release of anger. I said, "Yes, life is not fair, and you feel angry. You're angry at God, aren't you?"

Without hesitation, she burst forth, "Yes, I'm angry at God. Where is He? How could He do this to me?"

I held her hand, and I told her it was okay to be angry. Life was not fair.

Then I said very little. I just held her for a while.

After the anger subsided, she continued to talk, and again she repeated, "I feel so empty."

She wanted desperately to feel something inside of her, and that something she was calling God.

Where was God? How could she feel Him inside of her?

I needed to find out, was it something she had and lost, or was it something she was attempting to discover for the first time?

I knew I had not seen her at services. I asked if she used to belong to a temple. Did she used to go to services?

Yes, once a year on the High Holidays she would attend a Reform temple in Manhattan. But, she quickly added, the last fifteen years here in Florida, "I have been a member of Hadassah."

Only with ultimate willpower could I withhold the thought that went flashing through my mind. Fifteen years of Hadassah, of bazaars and meetings—did she really expect to find God and spirituality there?

I realized God had never really developed in her. How could I teach her the line of the psalmist, who said,

The Lord is near to all who call Him,
to all who call Him with sincerity.

How could she understand that God couldn't be inside of her until she called for Him, until she worked at letting Him in? Once inside, like any muscle, it had to be worked, it had to be exercised, it had to develop and grow to be effective.

For seventy-three years of her living, God was there all the time. He was available for support, for help, for encouragement. God could have given her the feeling of fullness that she now craved, instead of the emptiness that she felt.

But times were good, and she was healthy and happy. She had no need to invite Him in. Now, when she needed Him the most, when she wanted Him the most, she felt empty. But it's never too late. *The Lord is near to all who call Him, to all who call Him with sincerity.* As long as you're able to call, there's still hope, there's still the chance of feeling His presence, His closeness, His help and support.

I gave her and her husband a prescription, Together they were to pass the days reading Psalms together, to feel the pain and the hope of the psalmist, and to gain inspiration from it.

Then they were to pick up a prayer book and to pray. For then they certainly would be calling to Him, *with sincerity.*

— CHAPTER 9 —

Ticket to Heaven

There was a film made years ago that I believe is one of the best films about the dangers of cults. The film was called *A Ticket To Heaven*. An interesting title.

Have you ever wondered what a ticket to heaven would be? Virtually every religion has one. Some are general-admission, some are very specific.

I remember as a young college student being sent to speak to a Catholic parochial high school class. The subject was the modern Jewish observance of the Passover. It was a Bible class that was studying the Book of Exodus. They thought it would be interesting for the students to hear the modern end product of the ancient text they were studying. After the talk, there was the usual question-and-answer session. One of the questions was on the Jewish belief in the afterlife.

I explained that we had one, of course, but that to Jews it was not all that important. That our emphasis was on this world and making it a better place to be. What would come after was like dessert. It was enjoyable and looked forward to, but the restaurant was chosen for the main course, not the final course. The priest in charge was aghast.

"If," he explained "I did not believe in heaven and hell, I

would have no reason to exist." This whole existence was to earn a place in the next world. This life truly was a "ticket to heaven."

If I asked you to close your eyes and to think for a while on this issue, what would you come up with? What do you think are the necessary prerequisites to earn a place in the world to come?

The psalmist pondered that question a long time ago, and gave us his list in Psalm 15.

> *. . . Who will dwell upon Your holy mountain?*
> *He who walks in wholehearted integrity*
> *and deals righteously*
> *and speaks truth in his heart.*
> *He who has no slander on his tongue,*
> *who has done his friend no evil*
> *nor cast disgrace upon his fellow man;*
> *in whose eyes a vile person is despised,*
> *and those who fear God he honors;*
> *when an oath proves to be harmful to himself,*
> *he does not change it.*
> *He does not loan money at interest*
> *nor does he take bribes against the innocent;*
> *whoever does these things*
> *will never be shaken.* (vs. 1-5)

Is that even close to what your list looked like? How many assumed that at least somewhere in the list would be saying your prayers, following the rules, fulfilling the rituals? This is truly an ethical list, but where's the religion?

Some of your basic atheist types could easily make the grade. A serious ethical humanist would have no difficulty fulfilling this passage. It's probably a good thing he doesn't believe in heaven and hell, your basic religionist must be thinking, otherwise he'd make it in, and where's the justice in that?

What's the point of following all those rules, going to church/mosque/synagogue on a regular basis if it's not on the list? There's no confessional, no Sabbath; why, there's not even a sacrificial offering mentioned at a time in history when animal sacrifices in the temple were the ultimate religious expression. How could this list be the ticket to heaven?

The question actually reflects an age-old debate over the two parts of religion. Everyone agrees to the moral and ethical part. Each religious tradition has more in common than is dissimilar as it relates to treating our fellow man.

It is always argued by the nonreligious that they are as good or better than the religious, as long as they follow these ethical rules. To some extent they may even be right, but . . .

Religion is certainly about ethics. It certainly is about how we treat our fellow human being. Ethics are the cornerstone of all systems. But the religious person has an enhancement built into the system that assures a wider and more consistent following. Religion offers color to the picture, flavor to the meal, and pleasure to the task. Look at food and nourishment as a similar model.

All people need a certain amount of calories to exist. The body doesn't care how we take those calories in, as long as they are available to meet the energy needs of life. We can take them orally in liquid forms, or through an IV drip, or we could eat the same cold assemblage of tasteless mush each day. As long as we sustain the requisite amount, we will support life indefinitely. There will be no joy in eating, no enthusiasm in consumption, no break from the boredom. But we will live on. We will assuredly tire of the process, even lose weight because of the absence of pleasure, but we will sustain the minimum needed to survive.

Contrast that with a different model, in which all the necessary calories and nutrients are available exclusively in gourmet meals. If each time you sat down to eat, ostensibly for the purpose of nutritional survival, and the food was divine, would the pleasure not bring you back for more?

Your return would be assured, not because you had to, but because you wanted to. The enhancement of your life by the pleasure of eating would guarantee an enthusiastic and regular renewal of this activity.

If you could get your daily nutritional needs satisfied in a tasteless shake or in a pizza from a wood-burning oven, which would you prefer?

Ethics are the key to life. Ethical behavior is the sine qua non of societal existence. Ethics are our nutrients for survival. Rituals are the pizza pie that delivers those nutrients and makes us want to come back for more.

The psalmist is correct in telling us that the honest, caring person who helps his fellow man is on his way to heaven. But the person whose life is enhanced with many special and regular events, who celebrates his annual Christmas with goodwill to all, or one of the faithful who acknowledges Allah five times a day, or the person who celebrates freedom with a Passover Seder, is likely to find the pleasure in following the "goodly way" all the days of his life. In the end more of them will have earned their "ticket to heaven." They are the ones *who will dwell upon Your holy mountain.*

— CHAPTER 10 —

Parents–Are They the Problem?

Everyone is familiar with the perpetual jokes about men and women. The usual male mantra: "Women, can't live with them, can't live without them." The number of books, plays, and movies on the battle of the sexes is never-ending, yet when compared to child-rearing, the conflict and lack of understanding seem tame. Parents are forever complaining about their children, and children have blamed all of life's misfortune on their parents. A few humorous stories to illustrate the two positions.

Four women are sitting around the table playing cards. The first says, "Oy." The second says, "Oy vey." The third says, "Oy veys mir." The fourth says, "Girls, I thought we all promised not to talk about the children."

The other side of the coin is seen by the following two items.

Mrs. Goldfarb takes her little boy to the beach, and as soon as she settles under an umbrella, the routine begins:

"Alan, come here. Don't go into the water, you'll drown!"

"Alan, don't play in the sand. It'll get in your eyes."

"Alan, come out of the sun. You'll get sunstroke!"

"Oy, vey, such a nervous child!"

Of course that child grows up and becomes Woody Allen and then spends the rest of his life in therapy to undo the curses of his upbringing. Indeed, it has been stated that "Psychiatry enables us to correct our faults by confessing our parents' shortcomings" (Laurence Peter, *The American Rabbi*, April 1995, p. 14).

From the time we are little, our parents seem to be the benevolent giants. If they are home we are safe and secure. Their touch, their hug, their encouraging word is authoritative and believable. At times it is the most powerful medicine in the world.

One prominent pediatrician has a standard treatment for children who are prone to getting sick. On a sheet from his prescription pad, the doctor writes his prescription and hands it directly to the parents: "One hug administered directly at least once every three hours."

As a child I remember having difficulty falling asleep on Sunday nights. It doesn't take a Doctor Freud to figure out why. Sunday meant the pressures of school were to begin anew in the morning. If my parents were home on Sunday, it was somehow a manageable fear, but if they were out for the evening, the anxiety level was higher and more difficult to overcome. My parents certainly were not coming to school with me. They were not going to take the tests or deal with the class bully, yet their very presence at home lent an air of comfort and peace to me. I always assumed that this was a given. After all, we are, in the final analysis, products of nature. Is it not the way of the world that the mother cares for her young? Who would want to mess with a bear cub's mother? Lions are frightening enough without going after the space of a newborn lion cub. Of course parents are there for us—or are they?

It is quite shocking to see the "other side" of nature. Those who have aquariums quickly learn which species of mother and offspring need to be separated after birth lest the child prove to be a tasty morsel for the parents' dinner. The universality of parents as protectors and nurturers can no longer be taken for granted. Perhaps it never could.

Psalm 27 is a powerful statement of trust in the goodness of God. It is a masterful articulation of the confidence we can have in life no matter what happens, as long as we continue a trust and certainty in God's protective presence. He begins:

The Lord is my light and my salvation; whom shall I fear?
The Lord is the strength of my life; of whom shall I be afraid? (vs.1)

. . . If an army should encamp against me,
my heart would not fear;
if war were to rise against me,
in this I trust.
One thing I request of the Lord:
only that shall I seek:
that I may dwell in the house of the Lord
all the days of my life. (vs. 3-4)

He pleads for God's continued presence. No matter what life throws at him, he can handle it. As long as he is reassured that God will be there with him through the worst of it, he will survive.

To show how serious he is, and using language filled with almost unbearable pathos, he gives an example of the cruelest, most painful trauma that can occur.

. . . do not forsake me, do not abandon me,
O God my deliverer.
Though my father and mother abandon me,
the Lord will take me in. (vs. 9, 10)
. . . Look to the Lord;
be strong and of good courage!
Look to the Lord. (vs. 14)

Parental abandonment takes place in many different ways, but the trauma left behind has a haunting similarity. The common and usual examples of parental child abuse need not be overly elaborated. Daily we hear of incest, of physical beatings sometimes leading to fatalities. We hear of drunken attacks, and not only by fathers. We hear of cocaine babies born to strung-out mothers. We even have new diseases to describe the barbarism of the maternal abuse. "Munchhausen by proxy" sounds like a cartoon or a new Monty Python movie but is really a disturbing illness in which a mother beats her child in order to nurse it back to health.

There are other forms of child abuse not as blatant and not physical, but damaging nevertheless. There are parents who have stolen childhood from their children. Usually as an extension of their own egos, they want to make sure the children succeed in the world and do everything in their power to grasp some form of advantage over everyone else.

In early-childhood centers around the country, parents beg, lie, cajole, or bribe their way into a program for their child who is too young or ill-equipped to legitimately attend. They ignore the counsel of trained educators if they feel that a certain class or a particular teacher will suit their child. The decision, after all, of which Mommy and Me teacher guides their child might bear significantly on the application to Harvard some fifteen years later. In households like this, is it any wonder that love ultimately will be conditional and based on performance?

These are the parents who communicate a message of conditional love that ties academic achievement to parental love. "Get an A on your exam and then I love you, get a B and incur my disappointment and the withholding of my love."

We are entrusted as parents with more than the care of our children's bodies. We are the builders of their esteem. Today, in North America at least, the absence of self-esteem is continually cited as the reason for academic and social failure of so many youngsters. As Dr. Bernie Siegel has said, "Too many children get everything they want and nothing they need. The message to whisper in your child's ear is simply, 'I love you unconditionally (not if you get an A, or become a doctor). Life is full of hurdles, but whatever happens, you'll overcome.' Then give them some discipline, not punishment" (Bernie Siegel, *Love, Medicine and Miracles*, 1988, p. 223).

Parents have no patience for their children's childhood. It stands in the way of their performance. Rather than let them grow as children, they are treated as mini-adults.

Lucinda Franks, writing in the *New York Times Magazine* (10-10-93), notes: "As we hover over their development as though we were tending orchids in a greenhouse, are we not also guilty of a kind of neglect? In integrating them into our daily lives, have we taken away their freedom to do childish things? Parents or nannies of old stayed at home and babbled and played games; we take them to department stores, to work, to lunch, to movies and plays. Parents push for intimacy so much that one child was overheard telling her mother, 'If you say I can have my feelings one more time, I'm going to throw up.' "

I don't know what the exact form of abandonment was that the psalmist was writing about. I suspect it was the kind of cold shoulder that some have received in adulthood when we have disappointed our parents. It may be in the choice of a mate, a religion, or an occupation, but in the end the pain, isolation and loneliness are the same. We can try for a reconciliation, but it is likely to be doomed if they have invoked it upon us.

The poet Elizabeth Barret Browning's parents disapproved so strongly of her marriage to Robert that they disowned her. Almost weekly, Elizabeth wrote loving letters to her mother and father asking for a reconciliation. They never once replied. After ten years of letter writing, Elizabeth received a huge box in the mail. She opened it. To her dismay and heartbreak, the box contained all of her letters to her parents. Not one of them had ever been opened!

Had her parents opened and read only a few of them, a reconciliation might have been effected. But it wasn't, and it is to such a situation that our psalmist is condemned. Yet as we see, he survives and maintains his balance. His pain is palpable, but he bears it in stride, because he feels the presence of God with him in life. Note that he accepts that having God with him does not mean being spared life's pains and difficulties. He just feels that with God he can bear it.

Look to the Lord;
be strong and of good courage!
Look to the Lord.

CHAPTER 11

The Lord Is My Shepherd

Irving Stone wrote a novel about the life of Michelangelo called *The Agony and the Ecstacy*. The truth is, you don't have to be a Michelangelo to have that range of experience. You just have to have lived. There is no such thing as life filled with just pleasantness or filled with only suffering. Everyone is given a measure of both, and how we handle it determines in a large way the quality of the life that we live.

I've often taught that life is really traveling from one mountaintop to another while going through deep valleys in between. A charmed life has many mountaintops, and few and very narrow valleys. A difficult life has few mountain peaks, separated by very wide valleys.

Most people never reflect on the totality of the voyage but respond only from the position they are in at that time. Some arrogantly and falsely assume that the mountain peak is their exclusive domain. Others bemoan their stay in the valley as a permanent curse. The truth escapes both and negatively affects the quality of their sojourn on this earth.

Psalm 22 has one of the saddest expressions of despair that I have ever read. It reflects a combination of suffering from one who was always on the mountain, but who, by the end of his collapse into the valley, sounds like one who has been in that valley for a very long time.

One of the ironies of the human condition is that it is easier to live with never having had, than it is to have had and to have lost it.

I have perhaps the world's worst luck when it comes to investing in the stock market. I have joked to my friends that if they want to become rich, they should wait until I have bought a stock and then sell it immediately. If I sell, it is a sure sign that they should buy. I don't do it often (thank God), but the pattern is consistent.

When I start with a certain amount of stock and its value goes up on paper, I have a wonderful, happy feeling. When it drops and I ride it down to the point where I bought it and then sell, I don't comfort myself with the thought that I'm exactly where I started from. I grieve the loss of the money.

Why should I grieve? After all, I'm no worse off than I was before I bought the stock, and I wasn't sad in that position. The difference is that I had and lost, and that was much worse than never having had at all.

There is a classic image of the stock market crash of 1929, with men jumping off roofs after sustaining losses of their entire portfolio. What is interesting to me is that the very poor, those raised in poverty with no prospects of anything but a life of poverty, were not the ones jumping.

The poor may have been the ones to pass by the skyscraper buildings and fantasize about having an office there. They may have read about the rich and famous and dreamed, "If only . . ." or "Maybe one day." That fantasy still fuels the billions of dollars spent every year on lotteries, and that fantasy is perfectly normal.

But the ones jumping were the ones who had it all. They were the ones who had been to the mountaintop and, literally as well as figuratively, built themselves a mansion on top. They assumed a divine right of permanent residency. They were what Tom Wolfe satirized as the "Masters of the Universe." When their turn came to dwell in the valley, they were not prepared emotionally to even consider it. Their depression was so great that even death looked like a more desirable option.

Imagine what it must be like to have had success, wealth, friendship, prestige, fame, position, and power, and suddenly find it is all gone.

During the last recession, I had to deal with a lot of people who had been downsized out of a job. These were people of mid- to upper-level management. They had worked for companies for quite a few years and made a nice living for themselves and their families. They were just entering middle age, which is frightening enough, when they were suddenly and unceremoniously cut adrift from every anchor that they knew.

Work wasn't just the source of their income (which was substantial and crucial), it was also their source of identity and self-worth. They had climbed the corporate ladder. In the process, they had been told how good and how valuable to the company they were. Their rise and their raises were affirmations of their success. Now detached by their primary validator, their work, and what had become the surrogate parents of their adulthood, the company, they went looking to the market to reconnect. New employment would reestablish them as the champions they knew themselves to be.

Imagine their shock and disappointment at being rejected at every turn. They were overqualified!

A "kid" just out of school could do their work, albeit not as well. But at half the price, they were a bargain to the now downsized and bottom-line company.

As the rejections continued and the severance pay ran low, they swallowed their pride and went looking for lower-level jobs, sure to find something they had successfully fulfilled in their earlier years. It was not to be.

Employers were wary of hiring someone so well qualified.

"You'll be bored doing this type of work."

"It's below someone of your talent and experience. We would never insult you with this kind of position."

Now they could no longer find work of any kind in their field. Some finally came to me for help, as part of their networking. Some were prepared to do anything that would at least put food on the table. Some were prepared to drive taxis or to be cashiers at the supermarket. Others could not even do that. They became depressed and immobile. They slept in, every day, getting up only to move from bed to couch to bed again. Crying was their other activity, after watching TV.

"Why me? I'm worthless. What did I do to deserve this?" was now their mantra. They "became" the author of Psalm 22.

My God, my God,
why have You forsaken me,
so far from my deliverance,
from the words of my cry?
My God, I call out by day
but You do not answer;
and at night
there is no relief for me. (vs. 2-3)

The sound of anger, the sense of abandonment, is so powerfully expressed here. He is all alone, aware that what he once had is no more. This is the source of the pain, the power of the anguish, because he once had it. He could taste it, and when it was gone, he saw it as abandonment. It was personal. After all, he had entitlement. God had been there before. Where was He now?

And You, Holy One...
In You our fathers trusted;
they trusted, and You saved them.
To You they cried out and were delivered;
in You they trusted and were not ashamed. (vs. 4-6)

If you were there for my forefathers, why aren't you there for me? The past was my security blanket, and now it has fallen apart. I have been rejected, and woe is me! What's wrong with me? After the anger comes the sense of worthlessness, the total loss of self-esteem, and the deepening of the depression.

But I am a worm and not a man;
scorned of man and despised by people.
All who see me taunt me;
they reject me with a curled lip
[and with] a shake of the head. (vs. 7-8)

Feeling as low as can be, and reiterating his sense of abandonment by God, he now becomes overwhelmed with anxiety.

. . . for trouble is near;
for there is no help.
Many bulls have surrounded me;
strong bulls of Bashan have encircled me.
They open their mouths at me,
as a slashing, roaring lion. . .
My heart has become like wax;
it melts in my innermost parts. . .
And my tongue cleaves to my palate;
and in the dust of death You set me.
For dogs have surrounded me;
as a lion at my hands and feet. . . (vs. 12-17)

There is only one thing to do if he is to continue. He needs to reach out to God. He needs to pray, he needs to connect, he needs to believe that he is not alone, that as bad as the situation is, it can never be so bad that life is not worth living. He needs to know that he will get through the crisis and, hopefully, be the better for it. Indeed, that is what happens in the psalm. He prays and experiences a transformation.

Rescue my soul from the sword,
from the grip of the dog, my very soul.
Deliver me from the lion's mouth;
from the horns of the wild oxen.
You have answered me. (vs. 21, 22)

Then, in eloquence and with a return of his full being, he goes on to praise the Lord.

What was the answer that he received? What message could have so fundamentally changed his mental state of being? Our tradition tells us to turn the page. The answer is Psalm 23, perhaps the most famous and well-known poem in the world.

The depression began in response to a profound sense of helplessness and loneliness. The recovery begins in the same place.

The Lord is my shepherd, I shall not want. (vs. 1)

If God is our shepherd, then we are His flock. It is the very job of the shepherd to take care and look over his sheep. To the shepherd, each animal is important; each is an equal in his eye. The animal can not disappear and will never be abandoned, because it is in the very nature of the shepherd to care for every single animal. God our shepherd will never abandon us. He knows that we are troubled. He knows that we are scared, and so He calms us down.

He makes me lie down in green pastures,
He leads me to still waters. (vs. 2)

When we were depressed it was as if we were dead inside. Being so empty and so afraid, we were actually open to suicide. So it is that in response to prayer,

He restores my soul,
He directs me in paths of righteousness
for the sake of His name. (vs. 3)

Even as we feel trapped walking through the "valley of deepest gloom" (literal Hebrew), we no longer fear our situation, because we are not alone.

Yea though I walk through the valley of death,
I fear no harm, for You are with me;
Your rod and Your staff do comfort me. (vs. 4)

We are relieved of our anxiety. We can feel the change. We can lift up our head. There is light filling in all around us. Our step is buoyant, not heavy. Life comes rushing back into us. We have our appetite back.

You set a table for me (vs. 5)

and even though it is

In the full presence of my enemies

we don't care. We can function in their midst. We no longer see only the gloom and despair, the failure and darkness. We're not negative, cynical, or pessimistic anymore.

You anoint my head with oil;
my cup overflows.

We know to a certainty that

goodness and mercy shall pursue me,
all the days of my life
and I shall dwell in the house of the Lord
for many long days. (vs. 6)

We now know that we will enjoy this arrangement all of our life, because no matter what happens to us outside, we are secure internally. We will never again sink to despair. We will accomplish.

In *The American Rabbi* (Fall 1996), Rabbi Harold Kushner tells of two cases in sports where someone was up and then down. One was mired in the depression of chapter 22 and never got the message of chapter 23. He never realized his self-worth. He never accepted that with a shepherd, the depths were never so low that he could not climb up again. The other lived his life in the midst of chapter 23 even while in crisis. He knew he had value and could never spend more than a brief time in the valley before emerging again to the mountaintop:

The last time the Red Sox were in the World Series was in 1986. I dont know if you remember it, but we had problems starting Kol Nidre on time that year. The Red Sox were in a playoff game in California. If they had lost, their season would be over. And people didn't want to leave for synagogue until the game had been decided. They were losing with two outs in the ninth inning, when California pitcher Donnie Moore gave up a home run to Dave Henderson that cost California the ball game. Donnie Moore never got over that one mistake. He blamed himself for his team losing. He kept wishing he could turn back the clock, do that one moment over again and do it differently. Two years later, he was traded. A year after that, he was out of baseball. Then, hopelessly depressed, he took his own life. He could never forgive himself for doing that one thing wrong.

Now contrast that with something that happened two and a half years ago in a college basketball game. A 19-year-old sophomore from Michigan, Chris Webber, made a mental mistake that cost his team the national championship. But unlike Donnie Moore, he didn't lose faith in himself. He said, "That was a dumb thing to do, but it doesn't change the fact that I'm a good player"

A year later, Chris Webber was the NBA's Rookie of the Year.

The Lord is my shepherd, I shall not want.

— CHAPTER 12 —

Sowing Wild Oats

A great sage once said that the past should have a say but never a veto. He was talking in terms of historical events and precedent, but I wonder how it would fit with human life?

The question came to mind during the unbelievable events of the Clinton impeachment process. While deciding whether to remove the president from office for his adultery (though that was not the charge), a surprising number of his accusers had to excuse themselves or otherwise deal with the fact that they, too, had at one point been guilty of some kind of sexual indiscretion. Indeed, the entire tenor of politics post-Watergate has led to an intense scrutiny of a candidate's past personal life. Many have decided better to not serve than submit themselves and their family to abuse. There has developed a form of tyrannical hypocrisy that seems to say that if you have a past indiscretion, you are not suited for public office.

Has anyone paused to ponder the impact on the country that such a notion has caused? It seems that today only saints should lead, and saints have been an endangered species since the beginning of time.

Moreover, what message do we send to our youth, who have committed acts that in later years will cause them shame? Is

there no chance to grow? Are their life options to be limited because of some youthful indiscretions?

We often talk of sowing our wild oats, yet it seems that those
same seeds come back to germinate again in later life, under the
malevolent cultivation of a political or personal enemy. How important is it to an employer or the electorate if an applicant or
candidate smoked marijuana in his or her youth? Is an adult in
his fifties to be forever burdened by a criminal act of his teens?
If so, do they not have a right to ask, Why bother to repent and
do better? How do we expect people to change and grow if they
feel that their past is a scarlet letter worn for all to see?

The problem, like most issues in society, is not new and is
certainly not unknown to the psalmist.

> *O Lord, I set my hope on You;*
> *my God in You I trust;*
> *may I not be disappointed,*
> *may my enemies not exult over me.*
> *O let none who look to You be disappointed;*
> *let the faithless be disappointed, empty-handed.*
> *Let me know Your paths, O Lord;*
> *teach me Your ways;*
> *guide me in Your true way and teach me.*
> *For You are my God and deliverer;*
> *it is You I look to at all times.*
> *O Lord, be mindful of Your compassion*
> *and Your faithfulness;*
> *they are old as time.*
> *Be not mindful of my youthful sins and transgressions;*
> *in keeping with Your faithfulness consider what is in my favor,*
> *As befits Your goodness, O Lord.*
> *Good and upright is the Lord;*
> *therefore He shows sinners the way. . .* (Ps. 25, vs. 1-9)

Already in the time of the psalmist, it was established that
youthful offences could be held against you. Yet it is a sign of divine compassion that in God's world, forgiveness was possible.
The mistakes of a youthful past would not have to hold you back.
You were not doomed to forever pay a price for an error in judg-

ment from your youth. If God would forgive, could you do any less?

There are many examples of change, but one of the most inspiring came from a young man who refused to accept that his options were foreclosed because of the mistakes he made as a rebellious young man. Indeed, his story is even more compelling, for he took on the very institutions that deal with law-enforcement and punishment, and he prevailed.

A young man by the name of Bob Young was sworn in as a judge in Loomis, California. Many years before, at the age of nineteen, he was a prisoner at Lompac Federal Prison. According to the American Bar Association, he is the only ex-convict to become a judge. He had gone to prison for stealing a credit card from the mail. He served twenty months in prison and was placed on parole for four more years. His father was a Pentecostal preacher, and Bob Young grew up in a tough neighborhood in Los Angeles. When he was out on parole in 1962, he joined a motorcycle gang, "The Galloping Gooses." The gang was involved in a fight, and he was arrested with the other gang members. They were all charged with attempted murder. The police wanted Bob's parole officer, Walter Lumpkin, to agree to have Young held in jail until the trial. The parole officer disagreed. He said that Young must be presumed innocent until convicted. They put Bob in jail anyhow. Reflecting on this, Young said: "I think the hardest thing for me was sitting in jail and knowing there was a guy that had put a lot of faith in me. I had let him down. I had disappointed him. It was even harder to face him than my family."

Subsequently, the charges against Bob Young were dismissed, and he decided it was time to "grow up." He had entered college previously but now began to apply himself seriously. A college aptitude test indicated that he was best suited to be a judge, a lawyer, or a commercial pilot, in that order. His guidance counselor told him to forget the aptitude test. With his criminal record, he predicted, Bob would never even get into law school. Nonetheless, Bob applied to eleven law schools. Each one turned him down. He then made personal visits to all the schools. At the last one, the McGeorge School of Law in Sacramento, an associate dean, Charles Luther, took an interest in him. Luther was also the son of a preacher, and he was also a motorcycle rider.

Young graduated from law school and passed the bar in his first attempt in 1970. He underwent a two-year investigation by the state bar to determine whether he had the moral character to be a lawyer, and he was accepted by them in 1972. In 1974 he joined the public defender's staff in Auburn. Later, he campaigned for the judgeship of Loomis Justice Court and, though some repudiated him as an ex-convict, he won the election with 52 percent of the vote.

On taking office, Judge Young said: "It gives me faith in myself, but more, it gives me faith in the people. I know it sounds like a cliche, but I think this is the only country where a person like myself could come up from where I've been and be what I am now."

Be not mindful of my youthful sins and transgressions;
in keeping with Your faithfulness consider what is in my favor,
as befits Your goodness, O Lord.

CHAPTER 13

Old Age–Does It Really Beat the Alternative?

I seek refuge in You, O Lord;
may I never be disappointed.
As You are beneficent, save me and rescue me;
incline Your ear to me and deliver me.
Be a sheltering rock for me to which I may always repair;
decree my deliverance,
for You are my rock and my fortress.
My God,
rescue me from the land of the wicked,
from the grasp of the unjust and the lawless.
For You are my hope,
O Lord God,
my trust from my youth.
While yet unborn, I depended on You;
in the womb of my mother You were my support.
I sing Your praises always.
I have become an example for many,
since You are my mighty refuge.
My mouth is full of praise to You,
glorifying You all day long.
Do not cast me off in time of old age.
When my strength fails, do not forsake me. . . (Ps. 71, vs. 1–9)

The psalmist is no different than the rest of us. He knows what it's like to be young and strong. To have full control of your faculties, physical and mental. He also looks around and sees older people. He sees the weakness, the diminished capacity, even amongst the better-off. He probably has experienced the difficulties of aging parents and maybe has said to his siblings or friends, "If I ever get like that, please shoot me." He knows that one day he, too, will be old, and he's scared not only of the physical aging, but of the social changes that seem to follow. He has a great fear of abandonment that might occur in his old age. He therefore prays to God specifically to help him deal with this anxiety. The prayer is directed to God, but the source of this fear involves a lot more than God.

The first great anxiety of all people is that the body will fail. We may lose our sight or our hearing. Our bladder may weaken or our heart may prove too frail. Our hip may break or our legs become unable to support us. As our bodily functions lessen or leave entirely, we find ourselves weakened, diminished, and ultimately ignored by society. This is what Shel Silverstein was warning us about when he wrote,

Said the little boy, "Sometimes I drop my spoon,"
Said the little old man, "I do that too."
The little boy whispered: "I wet my pants."
"I do that too," said the old man.
Said the little boy, "I often cry."
The old man nodded, "So do I."
"But worst of all," said the boy, "it seems grown ups don't pay attention to me."
And he felt the warmth of a wrinkled old hand. "I know what you mean," said the old man. (*The American Rabbi,* Spring 1998, p.4).

There is another, literal abandonment of the body that is truly feared by all of us, and that is Alzheimer's. To watch a loved one in pain and suffering is very difficult, but to visit a loved one whose mind has abandoned its body is beyond tolerance. We come and look into the eyes of an otherwise healthy person and see in them the deep void of emptiness. We hold the hand of our life's love. We embrace a mother who nursed us, raised us, worried over us, and realize that they have no idea who we are. By the time they get all the way to the void, they are spared the ignominy of it all. Yet imagine the time of transition when they experienced the process of decline and knew what was coming. This could give new meaning to the concept of terror.

Do not cast me off in time of old age.
When my strength fails, do not forsake me.

Another common fear is that we will live and watch our worldly goods abandon us. All of our savings will prove inadequate and we will be forced into poverty or worse. Stories abound of the elderly living off of cat food. Worse yet may be having to move in with and be dependent on the children.

There are a couple of old folk sayings that speak directly to this. "One mother can support nine children, but nine children cannot support one mother." Perhaps more to the point is the saying "When a father helps a son, both smile; but when a son must help his father, both cry."

I knew a couple who were blessed with longevity and, for most of the time, good health. The husband had a successful career and retired comfortably enough to take care of him and his wife. Over the years, the children needed help: a car here, a partial down payment there. They gave whenever asked, as generously as they could. The family grew; the children were successful professionals. They lived in large homes, vacationed and lived well.

When the grandchildren matured and needed to go to college, their children again reached out to their parents for help. It is, after all, expensive to send your children to private colleges and still maintain a comfortable lifestyle without sacrificing anything.

The grandparents were generous with all their grandchildren. The couple reached their ninth decade, when finally, medical problems developed. They needed live-in help, or they would be forced to go to an assisted-living facility. Any facility they liked was beyond their means. The live-in caregiver that would have let them continue in their home cost more than the cash flow their shrunken investments could provide. They struggled every day to exist, trapped in their residence.

Where are the children? Isn't it time for payback?

The kids can't help. They're saving for their retirement!

Do not cast me off in time of old age.
When my strength fails, do not forsake me.

The final form of abandonment is related to the last case but is infinitely worse because it is so widespread and common. It is the real fear of being abandoned by our children and grandchildren. It is not because they are mean or vindictive, but because they are too busy with their own lives to have time or interest in the elderly. They no longer need them for money or help. They are now perceived as burdens or obligations, to be tolerated at best, or ignored at worst.

There's a Yiddish folk saying that reminds us, "Only when a mother dies do the neighbors realize how many children she had."

I have lived in South Florida for over twenty years and have met many couples who were retirees. I know them from that context only. They lead active lives and contribute to all aspects of our community, yet I have no idea about the parental part of their life.

When they become ill and hospitalized, I spend time with them. I ask if there are any children that are coming to help. Sometimes that's the first time I hear about their children. Often, only one of the children comes down, or they do it in shifts.

The parents are more concerned about them returning to their life than staying long enough to be of help.

This is also when I first hear about the children that are estranged. They don't even come, unless the angel of death is expected, and then not always.

Here is a story that sums up this type of relationship.

There was a young woman, a brilliant attorney, whose father lived 500 miles away. He was approaching eighty and failing in health. He would complain to his daughter, "I do not see you very often. How about a visit?"

She would reply: "There are so many demands on my time. I have so many court appearances and meetings that I am really too busy to leave the city!"

One day, he called her and said, "I have been worrying a long time. When I die, will you attend my funeral?"

She answered, "I can't believe that you are asking this question. Of course I will attend your funeral."

He said simply, "Forget the funeral. I need you now!"[1]

This is an example of the kind of benign neglect that we all worry about.

If children can hurt their parents, what about the grandchildren?

Grandparents are one of God's special gifts. To be blessed with grandparents, who love you with their own unique kind of unconditional love, is a special grace. To have grandparents who tell you stories of another time, another country, is enchanting. They are the transmitters of traditions and of family lore.

Sometimes, if we are really lucky, they are the ones who establish our self-esteem, who make us feel so special that we believe that we can do something extraordinary with our lives. And we do!

They were there for us always, and in the end of their days, they are certainly entitled to love, respect, and attention.

In our world, most grandchildren don't live near their grandparents, and many fail to even call on a regular basis. Those who live nearby find all kinds of reasons not to visit. This whole sad dynamic was best described in a letter to Ann Landers.

Dear Ann:

You printed a letter recently from a woman who criticized her grandparents for being so self-centered and uncaring.

(They refused to babysit the grandchild—said they had earned their freedom and had lives of their own.)

Let me tell you my side of the story: I have taken care of all my grandchildren since the day they were born. I was there when they were brought home from the hospital.

---

1. *The Orchard*, Fall 1995, p. 11.

No daughter or daughter-in-law of mine ever had to hire a nurse. I moved in to care for them when their parents went away for weekends or conventions, and when mothers were ill or recuperating from surgery.

Now I am 78 and in a nursing home. One granddaughter informed me last Sunday (her first visit in two months—she lives three miles away and drives a car) that she will not be visiting anymore because it is too depressing. Another granddaughter quit coming several months ago because "The smell of the place" made her nauseated.

Don't these young people realize we need their love and companionship more than ever now? Why don't they understand? Will they ever?

Ann responded curtly, but right to the point,
"What a heartbreaking letter. All I can say is, yes, they will understand when their time comes."

Do not cast me off in time of old age.
When my strength fails, do not forsake me.

CHAPTER 14

Can You Sleep at Night?

A rich husband is driving along with his wife in their Cadillac, talking on the phone, conducting business. After a while he asks his wife, "Darling, if I lose all my money, will you still love me?" She answers, "Of course I will. I'll just miss you a lot."

The age-old conflict between the pursuit of material accumulations and the pursuit of inner peace has been with us from the beginning and continues unabated in our time. In 1998 there was a film, *Civil Action,* starring John Travolta as a personal injury attorney. In a powerful scene a the end of the movie, we find him as the defendant in tax court, where he is charged with not paying hundreds of thousands of dollars in taxes. When he replies that he is penniless, the judge, in a state of total disbelief, asks him where all the money is. Where were the many things we acquire along the way with which we measure our success?

Indeed, when we first met him he was a young and "successful" attorney voted one of the most eligible bachelors in Boston. He drove a Porsche, headed his own law firm, and was a media celebrity. He lived high, dressed expensively, and was truly a phony. He claimed he felt the pain of his clients, but we soon see that he was only interested in their ability to generate fees for the firm.

By the end, he has lost his home, his car, his firm, and his notoriety. Yet when the judge asks him where all the demonstrable signs of his success went, he does not answer. Instead, the camera does a close-up of his face, and we the viewers understand. We, who have seen him grow, know how he has sacrificed everything for his fellow man. We understand the look. He is satisfied with his life. For the first time, he has a sense of self-respect and of real worth that escaped him in the old rich days.

He has helped a community remove a toxic dump that has poisoned many of the children of the town. He has punished the insensitive corporations so that they will think twice before ever fooling with the lives of people to increase their profits. He has truly felt the pain of his clients and made the world a better place. He is a real success, though he was never poorer, and we know and he knows that he is a richer human being for the experience.

The psalmist had a similar experience. Indeed, he often struggled with the lure of material success that others had, yet he continually returned to the conclusion that spiritual gain was far more enriching than material wealth.

> *When I call, answer me,*
> *God of my righteousness;*
> *when I was in distress, You set me free;*
> *be gracious to me and hear my prayer.* (Ps. 4, vs. 2)

Not everyone was on his level. Others were interested in less noble pursuits.

> *Children of great men,*
> *how long will you put my honor to shame,*
> *you who love vanity*
> *and seek deception, Selah?*
> *Know that God has set apart*
> *the devoted one to Himself;*
> *God will hear when I cry to Him.*
> *Tremble and do not sin;*
> *reflect on your hearts upon your bed,*
> *and be still, Selah.*
> *Offer the sacrifices of righteousness*
> *and trust in God.*

Many say,
"Who will show us good? (vs. 3-7)

Unfortunately, the message is not one that people want to hear. They are not satisfied with spiritual attainment. They pursue the "good life." They want possessions, affluence, material goods in abundance. A life of peace of mind, of closeness to God, of fulfilment in helping one's fellow man is not appealing to them. The psalmist understands what's truly important.

Lift up unto us Your countenance, O God.
You have put more joy in my heart
than when they have abundance of grain and wine. (vs. 7, 8)

And then we see the real value that comes from a spiritual rather than a material pursuit.

Safe and sound I lie down and sleep,
for You alone,
O Lord, keep me secure. (vs. 9)

To be able to enjoy a good night's sleep is a blessing. To have peace of mind that comes from something more then how much I have accumulated or how much I am worth is the real prize. A sage wrote, "Peace of mind that is dependent on physical comforts and meeting all of one's needs is the source of confusion. A person who becomes used to having peace of mind only when nothing is missing in his life will be broken by unusual circumstances. A person who seeks peace of mind by having physical comforts is similar to a person who throws oil on a fire to extinguish it, or a person who drinks saltwater to quench his thirst. For a moment, it appears to him that he is putting the fire out or quenching his thirst, but very soon he will see that the fire is burning with more energy and his thirst is even stronger than before. When is having enough, enough?"[1]

---

1. Rabbi Yeruchem Levovitz, as quoted in *Growth through Torah* by Z. Pliskin.

Everett Matlin, the editor of *Investing* magazine, wrote an essay about the kind of competition that is felt by those successful executives who are on the top rung of American business society. He cites the example of Lou R. Wasserman, the then chairman of MCA, who slept on a couch next to his wife's bedroom in their Beverly Hills home so that he wouldn't disturb her when he rose at 5 A.M. to place calls to New York.

Gustav B. Levy, head of the brokerage house Goldman-Sachs & Co, was up between 4:30 and 6 A.M. every day to ready "my briefcase." He said that if he didn't get up and work, he would just lie there and worry, so he might as well get up.

A psychiatrist, Dr. Benjamin Wollman, who specializes in treating business executives, wrote a book entitled *Victims of Success: Problems of Executives*. He said that his business-success patients all have trouble relating to people, have difficulty in trying to relax, find it hard to do anything except their work.

He describes one brilliant businessman who is cheerful and full of energy in his office, but when his wife dragged him on a vacation to the Caribbean, he was miserable. Dr. Wollman writes about this man:

> His only pastime was calculating the possible income of the hotel owners, or the number of meals served in a week's time, or the number of spoons and forks used at dinner by all the guests together. Once in a while he occupied his mind figuring out the number of guests who used the swimming pool and the total amount of tips given to the beach boys.

The pain of life, motivated by the pursuit of materialism, is all around us. We see high stress levels, physical and mental problems, drug addiction or alcohol abuse as an attempt to cope, by escaping even for a short while. Some experience burnout and existential angst or frustration at reaching our goals and still feeling empty. The sad truth is that those afflicted the most are the least aware.

A clergyman was criticized by his leadership for spending too much time with the richest members of the institution. In his defense he responded, "You don't understand. It takes very little time to convince the poor people of the community that they are poor. It just takes longer with the wealthy ones, to convince them they are also poor."

The same lesson is taught in a classic Hasidic tale.

Two visitors went to see a Hasidic rabbi. One was well dressed and the other very poor. The wealthy man was called in first and remained with the rabbi for a complete hour. The poor man then entered the study and received from him a blessing that God should improve his lot.

The poor man then asked: "Why did the wealthy person remain in your study for a complete hour, while my affairs took only five minutes?"

"I will tell you," the rabbi answered. "You explained your problems to me in the first few minutes of our conversation. I knew quickly what your wishes were and gave you my blessing immediately. The first party, however, took an hour of conversation before he realized that he was as poor as you. The blessing I gave him was exactly the same as the one I gave you."

There are many wealthy people who are as poor as their materially less fortunate brethren. The outer veneer, with which gold and silver may clothe a person, does not always give inner happiness. Both these people were looking for greater satisfaction in their personal lives. Both were looking for happiness. Both were looking for a certain fulfillment in life.

The fact that one had money did not mean that he had found more happiness than the other. The opposite may be true. Being wealthy, he did not even realize what he was missing in this world. It was only through lengthy conversation that he, too, asked for the same blessing that the poor person received.

The sad reality is that trying to reach the top of the material mountain is akin to a dog chasing its tail. You just can't get there, because as soon as you are near the goal it moves, it changes.

If you want to make a million dollars and be at the head of your group, it satisfies only until you meet someone with $2 million. Satisfaction is a hollow feeling when it is measured in things.

A story is told in rabbinic lore about Alexander the Great. He once stood at the door of the Garden of Eden and shouted, "Open the gate for me."

They replied, "This is the gate of the Lord, only the righteous are entitled to enter." (Psalm 118:20)

He said, "I am a king. I am someone of great importance. Give me something."

They gave him an eyeball.

He weighed all his silver and gold against it, but they did not weigh as much.

He said to the rabbis, "What is the meaning of all this?"

They replied, "This is a human eyeball, which is never satisfied."

He asked, "How do you know this is true?"

They took a little dust and covered it. It was immediately weighed down.[2]

The eye is a wonderful gift. It allows us to see the universe. From the most magnificent sunset to the tiniest atom, it opens up the world around us. Yet that same eye can bring us to the height of folly as it pushes us through envy and greed to an unquenchable thirst for material possessions. Some have lived their life in such a determined pursuit that they have polluted not just their life but that of their progeny. *The New York Times* (9/11/83) told of the ultimate horror story of a life lesson taught only too well.

One retired marine captain did such a good job of teaching his children the value of materialism that five years after one of his children shot both the parents to death, two of the other kids dug up the remains of his body to get his gold crowned teeth on which they thought were inscribed the numbers of a secret Swiss bank account!

The psalmist saw and understood it, even then. Others might get their joy and satisfaction by having more possessions, but it is a fleeting rush at best. The more money, the more tensions; the more you accumulate, the more you have to be stressed out about.

He'll gladly take less if he can have real wealth, which is the love and connection with his God. Give him a life that is worthwhile where he can help others. Let him fulfill the wishes that

---

2. Talmud Tamid, 32b.

God has for him, and he will reap the true benefit: a sense of peace and a good night's sleep, something money just can't buy.

Safe and sound I lie down and sleep,
for You alone,
O Lord, keep me secure.

CHAPTER 15

Are You a Frog, or a Prince?

If I said to you that there was a connection between a circumcision and a memorial service for the dead, you'd probably think me daft. If I added to that the observation that in both cases, the participants would cry, there would at least be a partial look of incredulity.

That people cry at memorial services is no surprise. In Judaism, on four different occasions there is a formal prayer called Yizkor, when we remember very specifically our lost ones. To reflect on a lost and loved parent, a spouse of many years, or a child taken from us in its youth is more than enough reason to feel sad and to cry. But to stand at a Bris, a circumcision, to celebrate the arrival of a new life, and to then give him a name, is a time of great joy, Why cry? How can there be tears at events that mark the polar opposites of life, at both the coming of the new and at remembering the passing of the old? What is the commonality between them that would elicit this similar response?

The answer is in Psalm 8. It forms the basic text that introduces the memorial service, and it is the psalm that we give the mother of the baby to read after the circumcision.

O Lord, our Lord,
How majestic is Your name throughout the earth,

74

You who have covered the heavens with Your splendor!
From the mouths of infants and sucklings
You have founded strength on account of Your foes,
to put an end to enemy and avenger.
When I behold Your heavens, the work of your fingers,
the moon and stars that You set in place,
what is man that You have been mindful of him,
mortal man that you have taken note of him,
that You have made him little less than divine
and adorned him with glory and majesty . . .? (vs. 2-6)

A Bris is a very special and joyous occasion in Jewish life. It usually takes place at home with many invited guests, including family and friends. It is followed by a lovely meal and is a joyous milestone in a family's life.

When I arrive at the home in advance of the ceremony, I can predict with certainty that of all the varied characters in attendance there will be two constants. There is a father in a near-catatonic state who is dealing with the impending procedure, with which he overly identifies, by being in a state of denial. Then there is a mother in a hyper state of anxiety, obsessed with fears and doubts.

The fact that this is a four-thousand-year-old ceremony performed by a highly trained practitioner is irrelevant. Will the mohel, the ritual circumciser, take off too much? Will he leave too much on? (I've always been amazed at these concerns and wondered where the mothers developed a database for comparative purposes, but that's another matter).

The requirement to circumcise rests with the father, but the last person you would want holding a scalpel near the child is the father, so the mohel is his delegate. The father stands next to him during the service and chants a blessing.

The mother is invited to stand next to her husband but in most cases chooses to be in another room in the house (actually, she would go next door if possible, but it's not a very practical choice).

After the cutting, I chant the blessings that include naming the child, and then invite the mother, if she had agreed in advance, to read Psalm 8. She begins rather tenuously, starting to identify with "from the mouths of infants and sucklings," and then reaches

> *When I behold Your heavens, the work of Your fingers,*
> *the moon and stars that You set in place,*
> *what is man that You have been mindful of him,*
> *mortal man that you have taken note of him,*
> *that You have made him little less than divine*
> *and adorned him with glory and majesty . . . ?*

And the tears begin to fall.

Have you ever been in the country on a clear northern summer night? Away from the city lights, have you looked to the sky and seen the plethora of stars dotting the sky? One gets a sense of infinity, of the awesomeness of God's creation. It is at this point that our new mother truly realizes that she has been a partner with God in this act of creation. She, in her "little" way, has added to God's work. She has brought new life into the world, and sheer awe finally sinks in. She cries tears of joy, tears of euphoric release as she realizes the miraculousness of her achievement.

The psalmist is quick to point out the importance and centrality of the life that she has brought into the world. In comparison to God's greatness and His world, she could have been intimidated into thinking how insignificant man is as compared to the majesty of the heavens. Instead, she continues to read how God, the Creator Himself, takes mind of man.

This little bundle, flesh of her flesh, has been made "little less than divine." Who would not cry?

At the memorial service the liturgists have captured part of the same awe, but from a different perspective. We are not now sitting with a new life, a bundle of potentiality on whom we are projecting so much hope. We now gather in loss, in emptiness to remember a life once so vibrant, so powerful so significant, now a mere memory, a departed soul lost in the ethers. It would be so easy to ask what it's all about. What's the point, if no matter who we were, how rich or powerful we had become, in the end we are but dust to dust? Yet it is this psalm we read to show us that we do matter. That life matters because we are special.

What is man that You have been mindful of him,
mortal man that You have taken note of him,
that You have made him little less than divine
and adorned him with glory and majesty . . .?

God has taken charge and made us special. In almost every religion that I know, there is an understanding in some way that man is the child of God. If as in Judaism we call God our King, then does it not stand to reason that we are princes and princesses? Our life therefore really matters, during the living and even after. When we cry at the memorial service, we cry out of a sense of loss. We feel the emptiness. We can't talk, hug, or kiss our loved one. We never cry out of a sense of their or our worthlessness.

This psalm teaches us that no matter what, from the moment of birth till the last breath is drawn, we matter, we are important. We are all princes and princesses.

Here's a fun fable that says it yet another way.

> Once upon a time I was a frog.
> I really wasn't a frog but I felt like a frog.
> Frogs feel slow, low, ugly, puffy, drooped, and stooped.
> I know how a frog feels.
> Sometimes, even now when I know I am not a frog, I get frog feelings.
> The frog feelings come when I want to look intelligent but feel dumb; when I want to be generous but live like Scrooge.
> I feel them when I want to live with an attitude of gratitude but find myself filled with feelings of envy and resentment; when I want to be mature but instead find myself involved in petty quarrels.
> I feel them when I want to care but find myself indifferent or, even worse, wallowing in self-pity.
> Once upon a time I was a frog, sitting on my lily pad in a big beautiful pond, filled with life and excitement.
> But I was too fearful to participate, so I just sat there, hiding beneath my bullfrog face.
> Then one day a princess came by.
> Everyone thought I was a frog, but she could see the difference.

She looked like just an ordinary princess, but not really.

She was someone special, and she knew it.

She was the child of the King.

She could with one kiss change people from being slow, low ugly, puffy, drooped, and stooped, to being a prince.

She came over to me.

She looked down at this frog.

When she did, I just knew that she could never bring herself to kiss someone so slow, so low, so ugly, so puffy, so stooped, and so drooped, but she did.

Instantly, I felt like a handsome prince.

Now I go around kissing people.

It is so much fun to change those who are slow and low and ugly and puffy and drooped and stooped. The change is instant once they realize that they are not really frogs, but children of the King.

What is man that You have been mindful of him,
mortal man that you have taken note of him,
that You have made him little less than divine
and adorned him with glory and majesty . . .?

— CHAPTER 16 —

Captain Kirk and Evil

The comic strip characters Frank and Ernest had an interesting conversation.

One of them asks the other, "Do you believe in fate?"

And the other responds, "Sure, I'd hate to think I turned out like this because of something I had control over."

Is that how it works? Do we have no control over this life of ours? Are we just pawns in someone's cosmic chess game? There is the Oriental attitude that "Karma is karma." What will be will be, and we have to go with the flow, accepting the inevitable unfolding of the predetermined design that is our life.

This is a view I totally reject. It's not that I don't believe in an all-knowing and omniscient God. Rather, it is a trust that though God knows all that will happen, it is I who will make the choices that will get me there. This is perhaps the most crucial belief that we can possess: the understanding that there is a God in this world who desires that we choose only the good. That we have the opportunity, by these actions of perfecting the soul that He gave us, so that it rises to a union with its Creator.

That union, or at least the serious attempt at that union, is rewarded with what various traditions call heaven, or nirvana, or Garden of Eden, etc. In order for us to achieve this goal, we have to be able to choose good deeds from bad, righteousness from

79

evil, commandments from sin. To choose the good, there had to be the option of evil, and it was God's plan that we have that choice. That is what Psalm 19 is all about.

The teachings of God are perfect,
restoring the soul;
the testimony of God is trustworthy,
making wise the simple man.
The precepts of God are upright,
rejoicing the heart;
the commandment of God is lucid,
enlightening the eyes.
The fear of God is pure,
enduring forever;
The judgments of God are true.
They are righteous in unison,
more desirable than gold,
even more than quantities of fine gold,
and sweeter than honey
or the drippings of honeycombs. (vs. 8-11)

These verses are the first part of the equation. If man is to choose good, he needs a guide. He needs to know what is good, what it is that the Lord desires of him. Choice presumes both the knowledge of good and evil, and the opportunity to choose. The teachings of God to man, through the revelations given to the masters of each religion, are the source for that knowledge. To the Jews, it is the Torah. For Christians it is articulated through the teachings of Jesus. The Moslem finds it in the Koran, and for the Buddhists it is the teachings of the Buddha.

Every culture has its own lore, its own legends, but in the end, every culture has its teachings, which the Supernatural has transmitted to that people.

Inevitably, if people truly followed their teachings, this world would have been a much better place to have lived in. (Let us be sophisticated enough to differentiate between the abominations done in the name of the religious teaching, and the actual teachings that were subverted by the forces of evil and corruption. Shakespeare warned us in the Merchant of Venice of how the devil could quote scripture for his own purpose. Osama bin Ladin does not define Islam. He perverts it for his own agenda.)

The psalmist acknowledges the glory of this gift from God. He even recognizes that they hold the key to his eternal reward and therefore is meticulous in their observance.

> *Even Your servant is careful of them,*
> *since they guard great reward.* (vs. 12)

But there is a choice, and no one is perfect in making it! Evil exists, and everyone falters along the way. He talks to us about two kinds of sin. To both he occasionally succumbs, and from both he prays for forgiveness. From one, though, he asks for more. He needs something extra from God to be able to avoid it entirely.

> *Errors—who can comprehend?*
> *From hidden faults, cleanse me.*
> *Also from willful sins*
> *spare Your servant;*
> *let them not rule me.*
> *Then I will be strong*
> *and will be cleansed of gross transgression.*
> *May the words of my mouth*
> *and the thoughts of my heart before you*
> *be acceptable,*
> *Lord, my rock and my redeemer.* (vs. 13-15)

The first kind of sin, the first challenge, is inevitable and unavoidable. It is the accident. The kind of mistake we make without knowing that it was wrong. From that, our culpability is limited and our atonement, easy.

The second type is the real problem. It is when we know that what we are about to do is wrong and we do it anyway. Why? What is there about us that would cause us to choose the evil? Why do two people, in the same place and given the same options, choose differently? Two people at different times see a man drop his wallet; one runs over picks it up and returns it. One runs over, stands on it until all have left, and then picks it up and keeps it. Why could this happen to two brothers raised in the same house?

In my tradition, we have a way of explaining this dichotomy. We believe that God created every human being with a duality of forces. We call them the "yetzer hatov" and the "yetzer hara." The good inclination and the bad inclination. The master plan of free choice necessitated that every human being have the innate desire to do good and evil. Life would bring the person every opportunity to make the choice over and over again. The good choice would elevate the soul, the bad choice would estrange that soul from God. This outlook on the Divine master plan of life is based on three basic concepts.

The first concept is that these two inclinations come from God and are embedded in every person. The second concept is that both are actually necessary for our fulfillment. The third concept is that our role is not to banish or ignore the evil inclination, but rather to capture it and use it for the greater purpose. Let me explain each one.

In the first concept, the idea that good and evil are in everyone is best seen in the following Talmudic tale.

> Rabbi Gamaliel said to his servant, "Go to the marketplace and bring to me something good."
>
> "Yes, Master," the servant replied and went to the market place, returning with a cow's tongue.
>
> On another occasion, to test out his servant, the rabbi said, "Go to the marketplace and bring me something bad."
>
> "Yes, Master," the servant replied, and again he went to the marketplace, and again he returned with a cow's tongue.
>
> "Why," asked the rabbi, "did you bring a tongue on both occasions?"
>
> "A tongue, my Master," replied the servant, "may be the source of either good or evil. If it is good, there is nothing better. If it is bad, there is nothing worse."

So it is with each of us. We have mouths to speak. We can praise and encourage, or we can belittle and deflate. We have hands to move objects. We can feed the needy, or we can rob and exploit them. We have brains to invent. We can create heart and lung machines, or we can develop bigger and better gas chambers. The forces for good and evil are created in every one of us, and it is our obligation to discover and recognize which is which. Then we need to learn to accept their mutual importance. That both are necessary is the second concept.

Some people, accepting the given of God's plan, nevertheless wonder why they have to allow the evil inclination to exist inside them. This is the origin of asceticism. We see pictures of medieval monks bathing in winter in icy waters to freeze the evil inclination out. We hear of self-imposed whipping as a discipline to banish or at least suppress the desires that come from the evil inclination. In some traditions, we hear of the sins of the flesh as the manifestation of that inclination. That is not an approach that I would recommend. Indeed, it is, to me at least, a misunderstanding of the very balance that God invented man with. Call it the ying and yang, or the id and the superego, the person and the shadow. The basic premise is that we need both inclinations, to really work as fully developed human beings.

There is a Talmudic saying that if it were not for the "yetzer hara," a man would not marry, build a house, or have a career.

If it were not for very real human desires, we would lack the drive to do the things we need to survive and then flourish as a race. If it was not for carnal desire, the human race would have ended with Adam. Without sexual desire, there would be no procreation. Without bodily need for shelter, there would be no buildings or cities, no communities or society.

I learned this lesson best from one of the most religious shows on television—*Star Trek*. Though the spiritual insights and overt religious themes have expanded dramatically in the later incarnations of the various series, it was in the original that I first saw a show dedicated to the concept of the integration of the "yetzer hatov" and the "yetzer hara." There is an episode where Captain Kirk is split into two identical physical bodies. (They allowed for some different use of facial hair to identify the two Kirks.) The only difference is that all of the good part of him (yetzer hatov) was incarnated into one body, and all the evil (yetzer hara) was incarnated into the other body.

As the plot develops, we see that the good Kirk is an ineffectual leader. He cannot make decisions. He is indecisive and weak. The evil Kirk, on the other hand, is self-possessed. He is constantly plotting for his own needs, to the detriment of any leadership responsibilities he may have had. In a dog-eat-dog world, his entire focus is on ensuring that he does the eating and is not eaten by the others. There is no friendship or altruism. Everyone is out for themselves. They are vulnerable to outside attack, because all their energy goes into planning how to harm their fellow officers before they are harmed.

The lesson of the show is rather obvious. Neither the all-good Captain Kirk nor the all-evil Captain Kirk could successfully perform as the captain. Only the proper combination of the two could bring the desired results.

The evil inclination is not to be banished or ignored. Rather, it is to be channeled and controlled, and that leads us to our third concept.

The book *The Ethics of Our Fathers* teaches, "Who is powerful? He who controls his inclinations." This is the third concept.

We each have a dark side. If we give it free rein, it will gladly take over and rule us. This is what Stephenson tried to show us in his Mr. Hyde character. If we ignore or repress it, it will not go away. Instead, it will haunt us in our subconscious and eventually manifest itself in some form of mental illness.

Jung would often talk of the need to recognize the "saturnalia" side in us. We need to give it a controlled vent, lest it consume us from within and leave us depressed and perhaps suicidal.

Freud talked of sublimation, of how we process an undesired but very real impulse or need into a socially accepted vehicle. The classic example is the person with a strong desire to slash or cut up other human beings. The one not in control becomes Jack the Ripper. The other controls and channels the impulse, and becomes a surgeon.

The sage the Gaon of Vilna understood this long before the discipline of psychology. He wrote, "A person should not go completely against his nature even if it is bad, for he will not succeed. He should merely train himself to follow the straight path in accordance with his nature."[1]

---

1 Even Shlaima the Vilna Gaon's views on life ch. 1 p. 1 as quoted Pliskin p. 62.

The psalmist understood that the choice was his. He under-stood that while God could and does forgive, He was not going to intervene and stop him from sinning. Rather, in praying to God, he was reinforcing his conscience and maybe even his sub-conscious mind, to be in control of his Yetzer. By praying, he ac-knowledges the ongoing struggle within and his need to be in charge. Perhaps praying is like a circuit breaker that he can use whenever he feels that the evil inclination is gaining. In praying, he doesn't expect God to act on him. He wishes to pause while in the Divine presence and to muster the strength to control the evil inclination. Finally, in prayer I believe he taps into one other source of divine strength and inspiration. He knows that to do good is to please his Divine Father. He also knows that to sin is to greatly upset his Heavenly Father, and he wishes to avoid that at all costs. Perhaps this true story conveys it the best.

Walter Wangerin tells about an experience he had some years ago with his son. When Matthew was seven years old and in the second grade, he became fascinated with comic books—so much so, that one day he stole some from the library. When Walter found the comic books in Matthew's room, he confronted him, corrected him, disciplined him, and took him back to the library to return the books. Matthew received stern lectures re-garding stealing, from the librarian and also from his dad.

The following summer, however, it happened again. Matthew stole some comic books from a resort gift shop. Again Walter corrected him and told him how wrong it was to steal. A year later, Matthew once again stole comic books, from a drug store. Walter decided he had to do something to get his son's at-tention and to underscore the seriousness of stealing.

So he took Matthew into his study and said, "Matthew, I have never spanked you before, and I don't want to now, but somehow I've got to get through to you and help you see how wrong it is to steal." So Walter bent Matthew over and spanked him five times with his bare hand. Matthew's eyes moistened with tears, and he sat there looking at the floor. His father said, "Matthew, I'm going to leave you alone for a little while. You sit here, and I'll be back in a few minutes."

Walter Wangerin stepped out of the study. And he reports to us that he just couldn't help himself. He himself broke down and cried like a baby. He, the father, cried and cried. Then he washed his face and went back into the study to talk to his little son. From that moment, Matthew never stole again.

Years later, as Matthew and his mother were driving home from shopping, they talked about some memories of his childhood. They remembered the incident with the comic books. Matthew said, "Mom, after that, I never stole anything again from anybody, and I never will."

His mother asked, "Was it because your dad spanked you that day?"

"Oh, no," Matthew explained. "It was because I heard him crying!"

Our psalmist and hopefully all of us, don't wish to ever hear our heavenly Father crying. We say as he said,

> *Then I will be strong*
> *and will be cleansed of gross transgression.*
> *May the words of my mouth*
> *and the thoughts of my heart before you*
> *be acceptable,*
> *Lord, my rock and my redeemer.*

— CHAPTER 17 —

The Missing Footprints

Cast your burden on the Lord and He will sustain you;
He will never let the righteous man collapse.

(Ps. 55, vs. 23)

This line is intriguing. In the midst of a psalm in which the psalmist feels betrayed by a dear friend, he calls out advice. He feels that the righteous need to depend on God for their sense of strength and sustenance. If we put our trust and faith in Him, we won't be let down. The truth is that most of us have felt let down by God. Rightly or wrongly, we have all felt a sense that at some time or other, we reached out for God and felt He wasn't there for us. We endured alone, or so we felt. But did we? Here's a great story that could have come directly from our psalmist.

A man had a dream that he was walking along the beach with God. Across the sky flashed scenes from his life.

For each scene he noticed two sets of footprints in the sand—one belonging to him, and the other to God. When the last scene flashed before him, he looked more closely at the footprints and noticed that many times along the path, there was only one set of footprints in the sand. He also noticed that this happened during the lowest and saddest times of his life. This really bothered him, and he questioned God.

"Lord, You said that once I decided to follow You, You would walk with me all the way, but I noticed that during the most troublesome times of my life, there was only one set of footprints. I don't understand why, when I needed You most, You deserted me."

And God replied, "My precious, precious child, I love you and would never leave you. During your times of trial and suffering, when you see only one set of footprints, it is because then I am carrying you."

Often, in our most difficult times, when we carry seemingly unbearable burdens, we do not notice that we are carried by the love of God. Sometimes we also benefit from the love of family and friends. We are nurtured and strengthened by the many support systems that carry us, until we can once more walk on our feet, safely and securely.

Cast your burden on the Lord and He will sustain you;
He will never let the righteous man collapse.

— CHAPTER 18 —

Don't Worry–Be Happy

I must confess that there is a type of humor that I do not quite understand. I comprehend the jokes—I just don't understand why they exist. Here are two short classics of the genre.

They just opened up a kosher McDonald's in Jerusalem. They feature "Never Happy Meals."

A man went to the bookstore and went over to the manager and said, "Could you direct me to the book *The Joy of Being Jewish*?

The attendant said, "Is that listed under truth or fiction?"

The man said, "No, it's under mystery!"

Why is there this cultural stereotype that Jewish people are never happy, that joy is something that escapes them in their regular existence? The truth is that joy is crucial for every person of every race and creed. Joy is necessary to cope successfully with life and all its challenges. Joy is the magical ingredient that keeps us going in the face of insurmountable obstacles. The pursuit of joy fuels much of what drives us to accomplish in every field of life.

In the Jewish tradition, there is a wonderful story that shows the centrality of joy in God's plan for our existence. The prophet Elijah never died in the Bible. He ascended to heaven in a flaming divine chariot. As such, he is used in Jewish folklore as the herald of God. Often in Talmudic lore, he would appear and be revealed to select people.

The Talmud tells the story of a rabbi who was standing in the marketplace of his own city, observing the frenetic pace of the people trying to make a living. He wondered, "Is it possible for people who are so competitive and so anxious to make a living, to ever earn a share in the world to come?"

Suddenly, the prophet Elijah appeared in the marketplace. The rabbi asked him, "Tell me, is there anybody in this vast assemblage of people who is worthy of entering Paradise?"

Elijah looked about him, pointed to two men, and said: "Those two are going to enter the Garden of Eden."

Whereupon the Rabbi, in great curiosity, approached the men and asked, "Could you tell me something about your occupation? How do you make a living? What is your lifestyle?"

They were surprised that the rabbi would be so interested in them and their answer was very simple. They said, "We are comedians. That is how we make our living, but we do one more thing. In addition to performing for those who pay us, whenever we see a person who is very sad, we approach that person and tell him a few jokes in order to make him a little happier."

Bringing people a little joy and happiness was such a high calling, it would gain the practitioners a spot in the world to come. Joy and happiness are not accidents. We have some degree of control over both, but for many of us, it has to do with perception.

A rich Hassid went to his rabbi and queried: "I can understand and fulfill with love all of the Torah except one commandment, 'One should bless the bad as fervently as he blesses the good.'"

His rabbi instructed: "Go to the other end of town and spend some time with Hayim the water carrier."

The rich Hassid traveled in his carriage to a slum and found Hayim the water carrier sitting in a flimsy shack, his barefoot children playing in filth, all gaunt from undernourishment.

"The rabbi sent me to see how you fulfill the commandment 'One should bless the bad as fervently as the good.'"

Hayim the water carrier looked puzzled, "He sent you to see me? I can't understand why. I have never been given anything from God but that which is good."

Kabbalistic mystical teaching warns us that by wallowing in sadness, self-pity, and depression, we can inadvertently shut out of our lives exactly those kind of joyful highs that we all wish for in our relations with others. We are not helpless, passive victims of life, but rather, active participants in how it unfolds. The more we remain optimistic, positive, and joyful, the more open we are to receiving the inner peace and contentment we all crave.

The great philosopher and mystic Rabbi Moses Luzzatto said, "Each individual's ultimate level is therefore the result of his own choice and attainment."[1]

This is not an easy path. If it were, everyone would always walk around in a state of joy and happiness.

The real world is a complex environment of polar extremes, and we have the option of choosing. If we want really good opportunities, then there have to be really bad ones, as well, for everything is attached. Ours is the challenge of choosing and of assigning the right perception to achieve our goal.

The poet Kahlil Gibran spoke directly to this point.

> Then a woman said: speak to us of JOY and SORROW. And he answered: Your joy is your sorrow unmasked. And the self-same well from which your laughter rises was often times filled with tears. And how else can it be? The deeper that sorrow carves into your being, the more joy you can contain. Is not the cup that holds your wine, the very cup that was burned in the potter's oven? And is not the lute that soothes your spirit, the very wood that was hollowed with knives? When you are joyous, look deep into your heart—And you shall find it is only that which has given you sorrow that is giving you joy. When you are sorrowful, look again into your heart and you will see that in truth you are weeping for that which has been your delight. Some of you say, "joy is greater than sorrow"—and others say, "nay, sorrow is the greater."
>
> But I say unto you, they are inseparable. Together they come and when one sits alone with you at your board, remember that the other is asleep upon your bed.

---

1. *The Way of Splendor,* Edward Hoffman, page 125.

Sorrow and joy are inescapable companions, and when we accept one, we open ourselves to the other. The only alternative to experiencing sorrow is to live such a bland and emotionless life that we will experience nothing, neither joy nor sorrow.

The challenge, then, is to be able to see the good in all things. To learn to appreciate what we have. To extract the joy even when it is encrusted in sadness and pain. How do we do that? Maybe the psalmist can help.

A psalm of thanksgiving:
Shout for joy to the Lord. Everyone on the earth
Serve the Lord with joy.
Come before Him with exultation.
Know that the Lord is God.
He has made us and we are His,
His people and the sheep of his pasturing.
Enter His gates with thanksgiving,
His courtyards with praise.
Give thanks to Him;
bless His Name,
for the Lord is good.
His loving kindness is eternal,
and to every generation
His faithfulness extends. (Ps. 100)

I used to think that this was a psalm of praise for God. It was fine to simply have a poem whose function was to change our focus; to raise our sights on a higher being and to sing words of praise to Him. Now I see the psalm as that, but much more. The psalm is actually a gift. It is an affirmation of God's wonder and goodness to all mankind. By simply praising God and his greatness, we connect to it. We become a part of it and beneficiaries of God's grace. It is similar to a meditation. This psalm lifts us just by saying it. It is like taking a joy pill. Try it yourself. Say it over and over again. Allow the words to enter your mind and then your heart, and finally to ascend through your soul.

People in alternative healing use affirmations. They give you little sayings to repeat to yourself, to reinforce the results you need or crave. It can be like a form of self-hypnosis.

My son, when he was seven years of age, used to prepare for a test by "screwing it into my mind." That's how he used to express a process where he would focus and repeat over and over to himself the material or concepts he wished to remember. It wasn't just memorization. It was a type of self-focus in which he was in touch with his innermost self and affirmed his command of the material. Once "screwed in," it was a lock that could not be broken.

We all have ways of learning, of teaching ourselves and of controlling our emotions. This psalm can serve as a kind of circuit breaker in our emotional wiring. How often do we actually detect ourselves descending into the blues? Have you never been aware of fear or anxiety, sadness or panic slowly spreading through you? Have you noticed feelings of helplessness or despair appear and quickly overwhelm you? This psalm is a tool to break that cycle. Read it again and again as a prophylactic, or as an attempt to climb out of the hole of darkness.

To feel the greatness of God is to elicit an automatic rush of joy. This is what astronaut Edgar Mitchell wrote about the relationship of truly feeling God and the spontaneous feeling of joy that follows:

"What happened to me was that, as I looked at earth and saw the cosmos, saw the universe, laid out before me, with this tiny little planet and these millions and billions of stars and galaxies and galactic clusters, all laid out in such magnificent array . . . it was an internal sense of joy, it was a high, it was a 'Wow.' And I had the irrefutable feeling within myself that this is an intelligent system I'm looking at. That it is not, as we in science had characterized it, a random collection made from the random collisions of energy-matter. That there is a coherence, that there is an intelligence palpable in the universe . . ."

This psalm helps us to appreciate that the world we live in can be good. We must always remember that perception is in our control. We choose to see things as overwhelming, or we limit them to temporary setbacks.

There is a story of a man who once sent telegrams to twenty friends at random. Each message consisted of one word, "Congratulations," followed by his signature. After a few days, every one of the twenty people wrote back a letter of thanks and asked how he knew that something good had happened. The sender took it for granted that if we say "congratulations" to someone, he will find something for which to be grateful.[2]

Joy is in our hands if we will only see it.

A driver was speeding on a particularly scenic stretch of highway. The sound of a siren brought his car to a halt. He was fully prepared to take the punishment due to him. However, much to his amazement, the police officer opened as follows: "Mister, five miles back did you notice thick patches of green grass which separate your lane from the upstate lane?"

"Not really," the driver answered cautiously.

"About three miles back you came to a half-circle in the road. Did you see—even slightly—from the corner of your eye, the bed of beautiful lilies which have just begun to bloom?"

"I'm not sure," the astounded driver responded.

"And then, just a mile back, did you even catch a glimpse of the long stretch of the aqueduct which bounds the road on the right side?"

"No," said the man caught speeding.

"Mister," said the officer, "the State spends so much money to make this road beautiful so that you can enjoy the ride. Why do you rush and speed and miss all the joys?"[3]

Shout for joy to the Lord. Everyone on the earth
serve the Lord with joy.
Come before Him with exultation . . .

---

2. Rabbinical Assembly Homiletics Service/Bereishith 5754, page 26, Rabbi Ralph Simon.

3. *The American Rabbi*, Spring 1997, p. 41.

Chapter 19

Guard Your Tongue from Evil

There comes a time in every good parent's life when they have to have a special talk with their children. I don't mean the birds-and-bees talk, though that, too, is important. Rather, at some point in raising our children, we have to sit them down and crystalize for them what this life is really all about. What do we expect of them? What kinds of values do we want them to have? How do we expect them to live in this world of ours? Of course, if this is their first exposure to these values, the talk will be an exercise in futility. They should have seen you behaving this way up till now. Your talk is to articulate what you have been living and they have been viewing, without ever having formalized it until now. This is what the psalmist is doing in Psalm 34. He takes his children aside and tells them what life is all about.

Come, my children, listen to me;
I will teach you what it is to be in awe of the Lord.

Who is the man who is eager for life,
who desires years of good fortune?
Guard your tongue from evil,

your lips from speaking guile.
Turn from evil and do good;
seek peace and pursue it . . . (vs. 12-15)

The purpose of life is to be in awe of God and to live your life accordingly. This, he promises, is the secret to a long life of success and prosperity. There are three stages.
Control of our tongue.
Convert evil into good.
Seek peace and pursue it.

Let's look at each part alone.

Controlling our tongue

There is an expression that "Humans were endowed with two ears and one tongue that they may listen more than they speak."

Unfortunately, we see a lot more talking and a lot less listening in our world. Words are powerful, and they can often have a more devastating effect than physical violence. Not everyone has the physical skills to intimidate, harm, or threaten another. If the proverbial ninety-nine-pound weakling walks into a room and threatens you, the greatest danger is that you may choke laughing. But anyone can walk into a room, speak a few angry words, and set everyone on edge. Friendships of years' duration can suffer from a few unwarranted and inappropriate words.

How many teenagers have had their life adversely affected because of a few negative words said about them by someone in the popular group? How can any good come from comments that are inevitably fueled by arrogance, anger, jealousy, or a negative, critical, or cynical outlook?

A sage is quoted as saying, "The mouth is the quill of the heart," and it is explained that the mouth expresses the contents of the heart. A mouth that spews venom can only be the outlet of a heart that produces it.[1] The irony of those who practice gossip and slander is that in the end they become victims, as well.

---

1. Chafetz Chayim, in *A Lesson A Day* by Finkelman Berkowitz Artscroll, Menorah Press, p. xxiv.

Putting others down in the end puts you down even more. It thickens and pollutes your soul. Would a truly happy person put others down? The momentary rush of sharing a good piece of gossip is far outweighed by the damage you do to your own soul and your own perception of the world. If you are always putting others down, you are conditioned to a world of bitterness and disappointment. No matter what is really going on, you are only open to the negative. All you see are the irritating, inconsiderate, and imperfect people who make your world so uncomfortable. You become incapable of seeing anything but the flaws in others. This leaves you in a constant state of anger and bitterness. With this on the inside, is it any wonder that your mouth gives vent to that dark and unsatisfying feeling by putting everyone else down?

I discovered a teaching years ago that helped me understand what makes such people tick. It has helped me deal with the mean-natured critics that one inevitably meets in life. There are two ways to be taller than your neighbor. One is to stand on a chair or ladder and literally rise above. The other is to stay put, but dig a pit to lower your neighbor into. You have not risen one step, yet you are surely taller than your neighbor, but what have you really accomplished? Yours is but a temporary and hollow victory that is destined to fail, and deep down, you know it.

There are people who need to stand in judgment and tell others how bad they are, how unsuccessful they are, how unaccomplished their children are. That way, they can feel how good they are, how successful they have become, and how accomplished their children are. Yet sadly, deep down, they know how empty their life really is.

For the betterment of the world and for your own benefit, the psalmist teaches,

Guard your tongue from evil,
your lips from speaking guile.

Convert evil into good

I heard a talk once on the issue of controlling good and evil in our lives. The speaker quoted his teacher as saying, " 'The power of evil is greater than the power for good.' A friend sometimes fails to help you when you need him, but an enemy never misses an opportunity when you are down. A man may forget to compliment you when you deserve it, but an enemy never misses a chance to make fun of you. So, if you can turn around from negative to positive, look at all the good you can do."

There are those who love to tell jokes, but often at someone's expense. Take humor and go visit the sick. Cheer them up. Visit the elderly—give them a laugh. Turn the bad to good. Instead of gossiping, turn the same energy into a positive act. Speak only good about people, with the same relish that you spoke gossip about them.

There is a woman in New York who has a label on her phone that says, "This phone is not permitted to be used for gossip."

If words can harm, they can also heal. Words of encouragement can alleviate despair, inspire, and even summon inner strength to heal where all else has failed.

I visited a congregant physician in the hospital, who was about to have major surgery to eliminate gallstones. It was a Friday, and if they did not pass by Monday, he would have had the surgery. When I saw him, in between bouts of pain, he felt he was definitely on the way to surgery. We talked, and then I gave him some inspirational prayers and words of comfort to read if he was so inclined.

As he later told me, he began to read the booklet and soon thereafter, he passed the stones. Coincidence? Probably, but you'll never convince him.

A story is told of Leo Tolstoy, who was walking the streets of Moscow on a cold, wintry night. He saw a beggar crouching in a doorway with his hand out. Tolstoy reached into his pocket for some change but found nothing.

"I'm sorry, my friend," he said. "I have nothing for you."

"Don't worry," replied the beggar, "you have given me the greatest gift of all; you have called me 'friend.'"

If words of gossip and belittlement tell us about the source, so do words of kindness and warmth. They come from the wholesome aspect of human beings. From personality traits like humility, positiveness, belief in God, and love of one's fellow man spring these ennobling characteristics. One who switches from talking evil to talking good is transformed. Now kindness, compassion, and mercy become part of that person's personality. One's very soul is liberated to ascend and shine in the presence of its Maker. It is not trapped in the dross of gossip.

People who gossip may have a temporary moment in the sun. Everyone rushes to them for the latest nasty morsel of dirt, but inside, they know that this is not a person they wish to be close with. If they can gossip about someone else today, they can gossip about you tomorrow.

The person who speaks good of his fellow man in the end is recognized for his trustworthiness. He is the one everyone can count on.

Finally, to eliminate evil and gossip altogether is as simple as denying an outlet for gossip in the first place. The Talmud teaches, "Better no ear at all than one that listens to evil."

"The listener to slander is even worse than the slanderer, like the receiver of stolen goods is worse than the stealer."

If there was no fence to buy stolen property, there would be little or no stealing. If there was no one to listen to gossip and slander, we could eliminate it entirely from our human discourse.

Turn from evil and do good.

Seek peace and pursue it

Seeking peace I understand. Pursuing peace I comprehend, but what is the point of both?

A Jewish sage who devoted his life to fighting slander wrote of this verse,

"seek peace for your friends and pursue it among your enemies;
seek peace where you dwell and pursue it in other places;
seek peace with your body and pursue it with your resources;
seek peace for yourselves and pursue it for others;
seek peace today and pursue it tomorrow.[2]

He goes on to say that pursuing peace means we should

2. Chafetz Chayim in *A Lesson a Day*, by Finkelman Berkowitz Artscroll, Menorah Press, p. 117.

never despair if we cannot achieve it at this moment. Rather, we must pursue it until we attain it. Even if we are called upon to sacrifice our own material goods, we should do it for the sake of bringing peace into the world.

Years ago, my grandmother of blessed memory died and left her modest estate to her two sons and my mother, her only daughter. Though she had lived in her daughter's home for the last decade of her life, she divided her estate evenly between the three siblings, but with one exception. She had a dilapidated cottage that she and my mother had lived in every summer for decades. This she left to my mother.

Proportionately to the estate it was not a lot of money, but it caused dissension between the siblings. Understandably, it was more a psychological issue of "Mother must have loved you more" than it was an issue of the money involved.

My father, to his everlasting credit, decided that the tension and dissent in the family was an intolerable disgrace to the memory of my grandmother. It should not be her posthumous legacy. He assessed the cottage's value and out of his pocket gave the cash equivalent to his brothers-in-law on condition that the money go to the grandchildren. In so doing, he truly fulfilled the psalmist's injunction to *"seek peace and pursue it."*

— CHAPTER 20 —

Geeks, Nerds, and High School

Whether you have studied developmental psychology or are just a parent raising a child, you are keenly aware of the stages in life that you, and then your children, pass through. Is there a parent who hasn't been warned about the terrible twos? Is there a married couple that does not approach midlife with some apprehension? I imagine the anxiety a wife must feel when her husband of twenty years starts acting strange and, out of the blue, shows up with a sports car.

Gail Sheehy has made a career writing about the life stages she calls *passages*. Yet when it came to one stage in particular, she was so overwhelmed that she eventually dedicated a whole and separate book to it. She called it *Menopause: The Silent Passage*. Silent because of the paucity of public talk, but surely not insignificant. Its effect on the person and therefore the couple going through it can be overwhelming. Yet of all of life's passages, nothing is as frightening and painful as the passage I call "high school."

When I attended high school, I started with the misconception that we were there to learn. The game plan, as explained to me, was rather simple. You studied hard, and you did the best you could to achieve high grades. This, of course, was all a prerequisite to getting accepted to college, and the major (read profession) of your choice.

In fact, since I attended a small religious school for the first few years, this made sense. Then I had a trauma. For personal reasons, I transferred to a much larger public high school in the neighborhood. I went from knowing everyone by name, to not even knowing where all the wings of the school were. I went from an environment that played by "the rules" to one that had its own set of rules.

Academic success not only did not matter, it was a point of social ostracism. To study hard and to score good grades was to be either avoided, or in the worst case, hidden from everyone but your parents. You could contract hepatitis and be wished a speedy recovery, you could break out in a zit attack and be pitied, you could get mono and be looked at with a degree of envy, as it was assumed you got the kissing disease from overindulgence. But under no circumstances could you be suspected of, let alone branded, a "nerd" or a "geek." Peer pressure was everything.

I remember once coming home close to tears, complaining about how I wasn't popular with the right crowd. I didn't dress the right way, I cared about grades and school, and I didn't have the time for the frivolities of the "cool" kids. My mother tried to calm me down and comfort me with good and sage advice. She started in on the "you won't appreciate it now but one day . . ." speech. It was how all the values and concerns of high school, such as athletics, clothes, the right look, and popularity, would not be important in the later years. What you accomplished academically and in your career would matter much more.

That answer had as much relevancy to me as Einstein's theory of relativity!

The same was true about the message of morality that we received. Morality was always preached, but no one expected you to take it seriously. Shoplifting was already starting to be seen as a sign of being "cool."

Years later, my own daughter, while in college, commented to me on how "odd" her upbringing had been. She informed me that of her peer group at college, a group of bright, accomplished middle- and upper-middle-class students, she was the only one who had never had at least one shoplifting experience.

In some circles the refusal to join in on the basis of "It's ok, everyone is doing it" is reason enough for your ostracism.

There's a poignant story that tells of the generation gap in morality.

A teenager and his grandfather were talking about the facts of life. The younger man said, "Gee, Granddad, your generation didn't have all these social diseases. What did you wear to have safe sex?"

The wise gentleman replied, "A wedding ring."

That message to a typical teenager might as well be delivered in Swahili for all the impact it would have. When Monica Lewinsky was interviewed on British TV, as part of the promotion of her book, she was asked about her sexual behavior. Her comment said it all about the shared teenage lack of morality. She claimed that "her generation was in touch with its sexuality." By this, presumably, we have a statement that says that, to my generation we're into pleasing our bodies, and find issues such as fidelity, adultery, and home-breaking to be hopelessly outdated or irrelevant. The assumed inclusiveness of her comments speaks volumes to this concept of shared values, or shared absence of real values, that permeates her age group.

Indeed, the message to not stick out too far from the "real world" is not limited to school alone. It is part of a mixed message that is transmitted by many parts of society.

"Listen to what we preach, but when it really matters don't be a . . ."

I know of a case of a young man about the age of eighteen. After having had his driver's license for about two years, he had an accident. He was backing out of someone's driveway and did not pay attention to the car parked on the opposite curb of the driveway. As he turned the back of the car, he bumped into the side of the parked car. Nobody saw what he had done. He pulled back into the driveway, walked across the street, knocked on the door, and asked whose car it was. He told them he had bumped the car and left them his number.

When he returned home, he told his dad about what had happened, since it was his father's insurance that would have to pay. I don't know what kind of reception he anticipated, but I don't think he was prepared for what he heard. To a disapproving face he was met with, "Only my son could be such a . . ."

The search of an individual to find the strength to lead a

moral life against the weakening pull of so much of society is what motivates the psalmist to write the longest of all the psalms, Psalm 119. Based on a series of statements organized alphabetically and in multiple clusters, he repeats this theme over and over again.

He acknowledges at first the ideal situation.

Happy are those whose way is blameless,
who follow the teaching of the Lord. (vs. 1)

He unfortunately is not there yet.

Would that my ways were firm
in keeping Your laws;
then I would not be ashamed
when I regard all Your commandments. (vs. 5,6)

We now hear the pleading voice of a teenager who knows what he wants but needs the strength to swim upstream in his society.

How can a young man keep his way pure?
By holding to Your word.
I have turned to You with all my heart;
do not let me stray from Your commandments.
In my heart I treasure Your promise;
therefore I do not sin against You.
Blessed are You, O Lord;
train me in Your laws.
With my lips I rehearse
all the rules You proclaimed.
I rejoice over the way of Your decrees
as over all riches.
I study Your precepts;
I regard Your ways;
I take delight in Your laws;
I will not neglect Your word. (vs. 9-16)

All is well, we would think. He has a value system to which he subscribes. He recognizes that God has laws and a way for him to live. He knows that to be true to this system will bring him joy and fulfillment. In each succeeding module, he reinforces how valuable and wonderful is the way of the Lord.

Open my eyes, that I may perceive
the wonders of Your teaching . . . .
My soul is consumed with longing
for Your rules at all times. (vs. 18-20)

Or

I remember Your rules of old, O Lord,
and found comfort in them. . . .
Your laws are a source of strength to me
wherever I may dwell. (vs. 52-54)

So if all is so wonderful, why is there a psalm of concern here? If he knows what is good and pleasing to both him and God, why is there a problem? (And there is a problem.) It all comes from peer pressure and his fear of succumbing. Listen to some of the obstacles that are in his path to subvert him from his goal.

Take away from me taunt and abuse.
Because I observe Your commandments.
Though princes meet and speak against me,
Your servant studies Your laws. (vs. 22,23)

Or

Though the arrogant have cruelly mocked me,
I have not swerved from Your teaching. (vs. 51)

Or

Though the bonds of the wicked are coiled round me,
I have not neglected Your teaching. (vs. 61)

Or

Though the arrogant have accused me falsely,
I observe Your precepts wholeheartedly.
Their minds are thick like fat;
as for me, Your teaching is my delight. (vs. 69,70)

Just like the teenagers I described above, so, too, our psalmist is surrounded by the "cool" people, the princes, the trendsetters, the people of means and lifestyle who torture him. They mock him, embarrass him, and at times attempt real harm, all because he is different. They can suffer no one who chooses a different path. The true seeker, who goes after honesty and the laws of God, is to be scorned, mocked, or stopped at all costs. To fight this, the psalmist wrote this psalm, summarized best perhaps by a cluster from the middle.

Your word is a lamp to my feet,
a light for my path.
I have firmly sworn
to keep Your just rules.
I am very much afflicted;
O Lord, preserve me in accordance with Your word.
Accept, O Lord, my freewill offerings;
teach me Your rules.
Though my life is always in danger,
I do not neglect Your teaching.
Though the wicked have set a trap for me,
I have not strayed from Your precepts.
Your decrees are my eternal heritage;
they are my heart's delight.
I am resolved to follow Your laws
to the utmost forever. (vs. 105-112)

The process described by the psalmist is never-ending. If we, at any age, are to make this a better world, we need to stand up at all times and in all ways for honesty, decency, and morality. We need to live our lives in that way and constantly teach the lesson in word and in deed, so that future young seekers will find a more hospitable environment in which to live. The following letter to Ann Landers shows how we can all make a difference if we truly care.

Dear Ann Landers: I stopped at a convenience store on my way home from work and purchased several items that added up to $4.80. I gave the busy cashier a $20 bill. Before she could make change, her manager yelled for her to come to the storage room. When she returned, she gave me 20 cents change. I said, "Miss, I gave you a $20 bill. You owe me $15." She angrily insisted that I had given her $5 and suggested I speak to the manager. I told her, "I don't want to get you in trouble. Just give me my receipt." She did. I wrote my home phone number on it and said, "Be careful when you count your cash tonight. You may discover you're $15 over. If you need this money enough to steal it, keep it as a gift from me. Otherwise, give me a call." That evening, the phone rang. She was in tears and asked for directions to my house so she could bring me the $15. I insisted on picking it up the next day. When I went to the store, she apologized profusely. I said, "Neither of us should be sorry. We should be celebrating. We both know that yesterday each of us met at least one honest person." (*Sun Sentinel*, Saturday, October 7, 1995.)

Finally for all those in high school who still don't believe hard work will pay off in the end, rent the video *Peggy Sue Got Married*. It begins with a high school reunion and consists mostly of a flashback of the high school years. Of great delight is the fact that the "geek" of high school years later is the rich and successful businessman with the "babes on his arms" at the reunion. My mother's speech about, "you won't appreciate it now but one day . . ." came true, after all.

— CHAPTER 21 —

Chaos Theory

The book of Psalms is everyone's legacy. It's not just for rabbis or priests, Christians or Jews. It is source material for everyone's soul. I was reminded of this one summer when I was visiting family in Canada and read a brilliant column in the *Toronto Star*. It was by a Toronto writer and broadcaster named Tom Harpur and entitled, "The Links Between God, Chaos Theory, and The Big Bang."

He describes camping out on an Ontario lake, seeing other campfires and dreaming of ancient times past. In his imagination he saw Indian campsites of years past, glimmering on the shore line. He saw the muskrats swim and the Canadian geese fly, and the scenery brought to mind some new science he had been reading about.

When a flock of migratory birds pass through and are startled, there's a brief time of confusion and chaos. There is a whole lot of different activity going on, including splashing and crying out. The air is awhirl with all the happenings. No one could reasonably predict which bird will be where, when suddenly, order appears out of chaos. The birds start to move, and a pattern starts to emerge. In seconds, a full and graceful pattern emerges as the birds prepare for their next flight.

I had a similar experience when diving over the Great

Barrier Reef. I would hover just below the surface at the edge of a great drop. Looking down, perhaps 100 feet, maybe more, in the crystal clarity, I would see major schools of large fish. They were swimming in groups, but in no particular pattern. Suddenly, there would be a slight darting movement from somewhere in the pack, and in a blink, with a blur of motion, every single fish would somehow be in the right position to turn as one. This phenomenon can be seen in nature, in weather patterns, and even in the formation of crystals.

Even though we usually use science to help explain and therefore establish order in the world, chaos theory in physics studies the unpredictable chaotic events where uncertainty is the norm. Try to predict cloud shapes or the movement of cigarette smoke.

Harpur points out, however, that in this chaos, be it the movement of grains of sand on a beach or asteroids in space, there is a creative force. Just like the geese, there exists the potential for a quickly emerging higher order. It is what scientists call a principle or force of anti-chaos. From turmoil and confusion comes a much richer design.

He explains that this is what happened immediately after the Big Bang, which created the world and continues to this day. He then explains:

"I believe that God is the architect and the intelligence in and behind this incredibly mysterious and complex process. I believe also that what happens externally in the physical order, happens also in the raw material of our lives. After all, we are part and parcel of the whole of nature. In other words, the forces of cosmos (order), chaos and anti-chaos are also at work in us."

We all know the times when everything falls into place. Times of happiness when we have a feeling that everything is as it should be. Times of thinking, of insight and of joy. But then we have the dark times. The times of chaos, of unplanned disaster that unroots us. There are the sudden illnesses, the death of a loved one, the end of a relationship. It may have come from without, or perhaps was caused by our own weakness, lust, or folly. We have a sense of being lost, of helplessness. We wonder why we were singled out for punishment.

It's at times like this that Tom Harpur enjoys the book of Psalms.

He writes, "One of the things I like most about the Book of Psalms in the Hebrew Bible [Old Testament] is that the writer so often wrestles and sweats over this very problem. It's like what I described in an earlier column as a 'dark night of the soul.'"

Yet experience has shown me that, as in chaos theory, one can almost always see in retrospect that the chaos held within itself the seeds of a new order, about to emerge. It was not "sent" to teach or to punish or whatever, but it did hold a promise of better things to come. There was, one may say, a principle of anti-chaos deep within it which, had one looked for it earlier, one might have discerned them and so have gained hope and courage even in the midst of an emotional, intellectual, physical, or circumstantial "mess." In spiritual terms, the Spirit of God is always "brooding over the waters" of our primal chaos to bring new order—as at the first creation.

To find this is to know with the psalmist:

I waited patiently for the Lord and He heard my calling. He took me up also out of the horrible pit, out of the mire and clay; and set my feet on a rock, and ordered my goings. (Ps. 40, vs. 2, 3)

CHAPTER 22

Only the Lonely

God will arise,
His enemies shall be scattered,
His foes shall flee before Him.

Disperse them as smoke is dispersed;
as wax melts at fire,
so the wicked shall perish before God.

But the righteous shall rejoice;
they shall exult in the presence of God;
they shall be exceedingly joyful.

Sing to God, chant hymns to His name;
extol Him who rides the clouds;
the Lord is His name,
exalt in His presence.

A father of orphans, the champion of widows
is God, in His holy habitation.

God restores the lonely to their homes,
sets free the imprisoned, safe and sound,
while the rebellious must live in a parched land. (Ps. 68, vs. 2-7)

The psalmist is calling us to rejoice. He is overjoyed because God will punish the wicked. At the same time, he lists all those who will benefit from God's protection. He talks of the widow and orphan, the imprisoned and the lonely.

When I first read the psalm, I found the list rather puzzling. I understood the widow and orphan immediately. They are the classic Biblical references to the needy and unprotected in society. In a patriarchal world where power, money, and commerce were all controlled by men, to not have a husband or a father made you powerless against any abuse in society. To be (unjustly) imprisoned by corrupt and powerful forces in society was also a position of real helplessness.

To call on rejoicing and songs of praise to God for helping these people is clear and understandable to me. My problem came with the category of the lonely.

How could the psalmist link a lonely person, who was otherwise all right, with the absolutely most vulnerable and needy people in society?

What did he see that would raise God's help in ending one's loneliness to the level of helping the people who were really unprotected and vulnerable?

It wasn't until I heard a sermon by Rabbi Hazkel Lookstien of New York that I first began to understand how terribly painful and ultimately debilitating loneliness can be. First a humorous story.

There is a story told that on the sixth day of creation, as God was getting ready to prepare for Sabbath, Adam told God that he was lonely.

He said, "I need to have someone around for company."

God replied, "Okay, I'm going to give you the perfect woman—beautiful, intelligent, and gracious. She will cook and clean for you and never say a cross word."

Adam said, "It sounds good, but what is she going to cost?"

God said, "An arm and a leg."

Adam said, "That's pretty steep. What can I get for just a rib?"

The humor of the story aside, it does speak to the earliest known time of loneliness. Adam was isolated. He was in charge of all the animals, but he had no partner.

John Milton wrote that "Loneliness is the first thing which God's eye named not good."

Of every other aspect of creation, God would say "and it was good," but not so with the loneliness that Adam felt.

Personally, I don't know of any human being, married or single, blessed with parents or without, who has not had at least some time in their life when they felt lonely.

Loneliness is one of the great horrors of human experience. Nothing eviscerates us emotionally quite like the feeling of being bereft of human contact. Loneliness is like hunger, signaling to our psyche that our emotional needs are unmet. One person described it as "a desperate longing . . . like a hole or space in the middle of my body, a wound. I can feel it all the time. Even when I am with another person, it's there, sort of waiting to grow later on, when I'm alone."

Loneliness affects our physical health, as well as our mental health. In a book titled *The Broken Heart: The Medical Consequences of Loneliness,* psychologist James Lynch documented that loneliness is especially linked with heart problems. He says, for example, how divorced men die earlier than married men. They have twice the death rate from heart disease that married men have.

Of course, not every marriage is an antidote to loneliness. The great Russian novelist Anton Chekhov said, "If you wish to understand loneliness, marry."

Let's first understand what we are talking about. There is a difference between the concepts of "being lonely" and "feeling alone." Feeling alone is not bad. Sometimes it's very good. To be alone is to be by one's self, and to like it. To be alone is an opportunity to have time for books to read, for prayers to chant, for meditations and introspection.

Thoreau was alone at Walden Pond. Reb Nachman of Bratzlav used to teach that every human being should spend one hour alone a day to be with God. Some of my best sermons were written alone, at the cottage in Canada.

But loneliness is totally different. Loneliness is not something that we choose. Loneliness is when we want personal connections and, for whatever reason, we can't have them. Loneliness is the wrenching feeling in our stomach when we feel that everyone has rejected us. Loneliness is standing on an island within view of a distant shore. All the people are there on the shore, active, happy, singing, dancing, laughing, playing. You see them all, but nothing is close enough for you to be able to reach out and join them. (You don't have to be on an island detached from the crowd. I've seen it happen in the middle of a crowded room.)

Loneliness is growing up as a child, feeling that there is some kind of imaginary circle, that all the other kids are inside, and you stand outside, and there is no room for you.

Loneliness is a feeling as we look in the mirror and see ourselves aging. It is realizing that there is more behind us than ahead, not only of our lives, but of people that we knew. Loneliness is the fear, constantly growing, that we are going to be shut out. We are going to be left behind, not because of who we are, but because we are becoming old.

I visit nursing homes and see the people sitting on chairs, gazing off into the distance. They are surrounded by other gazers, often lined up liked ducks in a row, always looking off.

They are seated in a straight line, not a circle, never connecting in, at, or to each other. I remember seeing the old people on Miami Beach, sitting on the porches, rocking on their chairs in a daze, long before South Beach became rejuvenated. It didn't matter how many of them there were. They always seemed to be so lonely.

There's the loneliness of the single life, regardless of at what stage in our life we encounter it. The teenager whose friends have all got boyfriends and girlfriends and are out on dates on Saturday night while and he or she is left at home feeling lonely. The singles in their twenties, having missed the first wave of marriage opportunities coming out of college, starting their careers, surrounded by friends, but living an inner sense of loneliness because they crave the intimacy that they have not yet found. The survivors of a marriage that ended by divorce or by death. Once they tasted of partnership, and learned to experience life as "we." Now they exist individually, in a situation where every part of their past experience, including their friendship circle, was defined by "coupledom." Suddenly, they are cast off to sea, almost pariah-like, to float by themselves. Many end up wallowing in their loneliness.

What about the loneliness of marriage? Two people who once reached out together and who now coexist, but are alone? Lovers exist without love, partners bereft of any partnership, still together but with a decaying love. They both reach out for each other, but unfortunately, never at the same time.

Each trauma, each different situation, sends us back to feelings and emotions that remind us of that child, trapped on the island. She is looking out, seeing the crowd, reaching out, but not quite making the connection.

This is some of the pain the psalmist alludes to when he categorizes the lonely with the other vulnerable categories. Yet his message has in it an implied promise of hope. There are ways out of the loneliness.

God restores the lonely to their homes.

We can even help God build a bridge from "that island" back to the mainland of connectedness. There are things to do, and things not to do. The first is to not escape. There are people who want to avoid the crushing pain of loneliness by watching television, or they read or listen to music, but always to great excess. It cuts them off from the world of people. Some go into the escape of sleeping too much, of depression, or even of imaginary intimacy. They remember the lost relationship, or the deceased lover, who have become an idealization that never quite existed that way. Finally, the ultimate escape is to consider suicide.

A folk story tells of a miserable peddler, an orphan without wife or children. Alone in the forest and alone in his world, he carries his bundles of sticks against his raw shoulder, cursing his burden, his loneliness, his wretched lot in life. In the middle of his brooding, a gust of wind lifts his bundle of sticks and scatters them on the ground. He cries out, "Master of the universe, who needs such a life? Send the angel of death and let my misery come to an end!" With that, in a flash, the angel of death, in his menacing costume, appears.

He asks the peddler, "You called?"

"Yes, yes, yes, yes, uh, uh, could you please, dear sir, help me gather my sticks and mount them on my shoulders?"

Our answer to loneliness is not the end of our life. The first answer is to be with people, to find ways to get outside of ourselves and to connect. In Hebrew, the word for "life" is *chayim*. And it appears only in the plural form. *Chayim* means, literally, "lives." There really is no such thing as solitary life. There is no "I" without "you," no "me" without "us."

In life we are dependent on others. The way we overcome loneliness is not by waiting to receive a donation of companionship, but rather by offering and giving companionship and meaning to others.

So how do we alleviate our loneliness? Begin by alleviating somebody else's loneliness. Reach out to someone else and make them a little less lonely, and watch the wonder of how you feel. If you are lonely, care about other people, and in connecting with them, your loneliness will disappear.

But loneliness can be caused by other people who reject us. Sometimes it seems that no matter how much we try, how hard we reach out to our children, to casual acquaintances, to potential suitors, the result seems to be the same. They turn their backs on us, abandon us, refuse to accept us, at the point that we reach out to them. Did you ever wonder how much of that is caused by what we do? How many of us who have been rejected are judgmental of other people, or are negative or critical? How many of us are impatient with others, insensitive to the feelings of others?

A writer, Peretz, tells the story about a child who is constantly fighting with his siblings. His mother can't take it anymore. She scolds him. She says, "It's always your fault."

The boy is hurt. He is angry. He runs out. He runs into a valley and at the top of his voice he yells out, "I hate you, I hate you."

The echo comes back from the mountains on either side. It says, "I hate you, I hate you."

He goes running back to his mother and he says, "Mom, I can't take it anymore. The whole world stinks. Everybody hates me."

His mother asks him what happened. He explains.

She says, "Go back to the valley. Go sit exactly where you sat before and yell out, 'I love you, I love you.'"

He did, and, of course, the echo came back reaffirming it.

He came back with a smile to his mother and said, "The whole world loves me."

So many times we blame everyone else for what's happening to us. We don't bother to see that what we get back is very often a reflection of what we send out.

Finally, as the psalmist teaches over and over again, if you have God in your life, you can't really be lonely. You can't feel that you are totally abandoned when you know that you have a relationship with a God who cares.

People may reject us, but if we're loyal and dedicated to God, God doesn't reject us. People can ostracize us, can choose not to like us because of their own problems or because of their own inadequacies. God does not.

Moses was probably the loneliest man in the Bible. Time and time again, he was betrayed by his own people. His brother Aaron aided in the treachery of the Golden Calf. His sister Miriam gossiped viciously about him. His people defied him repeatedly, and it even seems that God had abandoned him.

God had forbidden him from entering the Promised Land, the one thing Moses wanted most in his life. Yet, at the end of his life, in the depths of old age, unable to fulfill the dream of entering the land when it was so close, he walked up Mount Nebo, to the top of the mountain, and the Bible tells us that he was not alone. "The Lord showed him all of the land."

At the very end, Moses was not alone, because God was with him.

No one has to be so very lonely. That's the promise of faith— we are never alone. God is with us.

So if you find yourself struggling with loneliness, remember—reach out to help somebody. Giving to them replenishes you. Don't fear those times of being alone. Use it to encourage your creativity. Jettison your negativity. With a smile, bring positive energy to the world and bask in the warm reflection. Remember, always, that God is with you. Let Him in.

— CHAPTER 23 —

Parents–Are They the Problem?
Part Two

Back in chapter 10, I addressed the issue of parent-child estrangement. As long as we have two parents to have difficulties with, I thought it would be acceptable to have a second chapter to look at the psalm and the problem again.

One of my favorite psalms of all is Psalm 27. In the Jewish tradition, it is recited every day for a month leading up to the High Holy Days. This is to prepare us for our intense encounter with God. The psalm contains some of the most powerful statements of faith, yet it also contains one of the most painful and haunting lines of all scripture. First the verses of faith.

The Lord is my light and my help;
whom should I fear?
The Lord is the stronghold of my life;
whom should I dread?
When evil men assail me
to devour my flesh,
it is they, my foes and my enemies,
who stumble and fall.
Should an army besiege me,

my heart should have no fear;
should war beset me,
still would I be confident.

One thing I ask of the Lord;
only that do I seek:
to live in the house of the Lord
all the days of my life,
to gaze upon the beauty of the Lord,
to frequent His temple.
He will shelter me in His pavilion
on an evil day,
grant me the protection of His tent,
raise me high upon rock.
Now is my head high
over my enemies roundabout;
I sacrifice in His tent with shouts of joy,
singing and chanting a hymn to the Lord. (vs. 1-6)

Suddenly, there is a change. Life is never smooth, not even for the righteous. Something has happened, and our psalmist is afraid. He calls out to God for support.

Hear, O Lord, when I cry out aloud;
have mercy on me, answer me.
In Your behalf my heart says:
"Seek My face!"
O Lord, I seek Your face.
Do not hide Your face from me;
do not thrust aside Your servant in anger;
You have ever been my help.
Do not forsake me, do not abandon me,
O God, my deliverer. (vs. 7-9)

Then we see part of what's affecting him in one of the saddest and most pathos-filled verses in all of Psalms.

Though my father and my mother abandon me,
the Lord will take me in. (vs. 10)

At some point in his past, his parents abandoned him. That trauma has scarred him, and now, in his time of trouble, he is worried. Maybe it will happen again. After all, if his earthly parents have abandoned him, could not his heavenly Father, as well? Then he reaches out to God and finds his moorings again.

Show me Your way, O Lord,
and lead me on a level path
because of my watchful foes.
Do not subject me to the will of my foes,
for false witnesses and unjust accusers
have appeared against me. (vs. 11-12)

His faith is strong and now reaffirmed. It will get him through.

Had I not the assurance
that I would enjoy the goodness of the Lord
in the land of the living . . . (vs. 13)

If he were not certain, he would . . . what? Kill himself? Perhaps. But he is certain as he concludes. He is totally together again, totally certain of the support of God.

Look to the Lord;
be strong and of good courage!
O look to the Lord! (vs. 14)

What kind of pain must it be like to suffer the abandonment by your parents? What kind of loneliness must he have had to endure? It's almost beyond our comprehension to imagine. Yet we know the classic tale of children left in baskets on the doorsteps of strangers. In our modern times, that kind of tale has become mild. Here is a real case as reported in the newspaper.

A newborn baby who was thrown down a garbage chute into a trash compactor narrowly escaped death when a janitor who was about to activate the machine heard him whimpering.

The four- or five-day-old baby, clad in diapers and tee shirt, was taken to Mercy Hospital for treatment of exposure after the discovery Friday. He was not injured in the ordeal, according to a hospital spokesman, who said that nurses had dubbed him "Patrick Joseph" in honor of St. Patrick's Day.

James Bauman, the janitor of the Chicago Housing Authority Project, told police that when he heard the muffled crying, he expected to find a kitten, and when he looked inside he saw an exceptionally pretty child lying on the top of the garbage heap. The police said the little boy apparently had been abandoned by his mother at the Dearborn Housing Project on the South Side.

They speculated that the infant could have been dropped down a garbage chute from any of the building's six floors. The supervisor, who asked to remain unidentified, said he would recommend Bauman for a special commendation. "He thought it was a cat," the supervisor said. "These guys don't like cats too much because they jump out and scratch you. He could have just pushed the button."

What could go through a parent's mind to do such a thing?

I have raised three children through teen years and have personally tasted the "delights" of teen rebellion. Yet in the worst of moments, I could never imagine abandoning my children in that or any way.

Of course, there are other ways of abandoning. I don't think our psalmist was abandoned in the way of the story above. He is all too much "together" for one who had sustained that kind of trauma. I think our psalmist suffered from a different, more subtle form. The pain was still acute and very deep, but the act much less overt.

Perhaps he suffered from a twentieth-century form of abandonment. The one in which the parent is too busy to give adequate time to the child. Children need time; they need to feel that they matter to us. We have to make them feel special to us, because that's part of how they develop self-worth.

We don't do a good job. We develop excuses, or self-righteous reasons why we can't find enough time for our children. It has become such a problem that we have been forced to invent a new concept to perpetuate the deception that we are fulfilling our parental role. We came up with the idea of "quality time." Now we can admit that we don't spend enough time with our children, but it's all right, because "what I don't have time for with my busy schedule I make up for in the quality time I spend with my children." Who are we kidding?

Here's a scenario that's much more realistic in today's world.

A young child, Joey, asked his father a few questions from his history homework which his father couldn't answer. The father wanted to get back to his newspaper, so he said, "Joey, I would like to know what would have happened if I'd asked as many questions when I was a boy."

And Joey answered him, "Perhaps you'd have been able to answer some of mine."

Rabbi Hillel E. Silverman once spoke on this issue and began by quoting George Wills, who wrote that "Our lives are measured by coffee spoons of small activities."

Elaborating, Rabbi Silverman explained that "he referred to a fascinating survey prepared by efficiency experts in priority time management. They came to the conclusion that in the normal life span we spend seven years in the bathroom, six years eating, five years waiting in line, four years cleaning the house, three years at meetings. We spend one entire year in searching for misplaced articles, and eight months a year in opening junk mail. Six months are consumed waiting at red lights.

They discovered that the average husband and wife spend four minutes in daily conversation and thirty seconds in discussions with their children. No wonder children feel lost and lonely. No wonder so many choose to act out that emptiness with attention-gathering antisocial behavior. Some parents are so much into themselves that they have no room for their kids. Isn't that a grotesque abandonment? How lonely must it feel to be surrounded, physically, by the same people who have mentally abandoned you?

There is another form of parental abandonment, also ever growing in our time.

Parents have a responsibility to parent. They are role models, morality teachers who, by their deeds even more than their words, guide their children on a proper path in life. Today, many parents would rather be their children's friend than their parents.

In the office of a child therapist, a 10-year-old girl leaned back and gazed at her mother with half-lidded contempt.The child was there because her divorced parents couldn't do anything with her. Her father was bitter because he had brought her along to buy his girlfriend an engagement gift and she had sulked the whole time.

Her mother complained that she refused to make friends with the mother's boyfriend.

"How do you expect me to have a relationship with him," the girl said with the ennui of a 40-year-old, "when he's always in your bedroom?"

The therapist shook her head when she recounted the visit.

"Sometimes I think I'm too old-fashioned to practice in today's world. Half the time the children act like adults and the adults behave like children."[1]

Finally, there is another form of abandonment that too many parents in today's world are guilty of. They deprive their children of a religious discipline that would serve as a moral compass.

Woody Allen describes such a situation in his story "No Kaddish for Weinstein."

There is an intellectual who "suffered untold injustices and persecutions because of his religion, mostly from his parents." Even though they are Jewish, "they could never accept the fact that their son was Jewish."

No less an expert than the great pediatrician Benjamin Spock argued that children need to be anchored through religion. Children at first worship their parents because they appear wise, powerful, and rich. When children reach about age five, they begin to absorb their parents' values. He stressed that if parents have strong religious beliefs, this simplifies the whole matter of giving religious ideals to children. It is powerfully moving. Idealism is preserved.

The problem is that religions, beliefs, and ideals are less central to the lives of many Americans.

---

1. From an article on page 28-30, in *The New York Times Magazine,* October 10, 1993, by Lucinda Franks.

We live in an open environment in North America. Everyone can and does marry anyone they choose. The incidence of mixed marriages between Catholics, Protestants, Jews, Moslems, Buddhists, and others has led to the "I'll let the children choose when they are older" syndrome.

In my office I counsel potential mixed marriages to choose one religion or the other, but choose something. Give the children a foundation.

If they choose to reject it in later years for something else, that will be their adult choice. For now, though, make a decision and put in a plan of action for them. I often point out to them what I call the "toothbrush argument." How many parents will say to a three-year-old, You may or may not brush your teeth—it's entirely up to you? No one, I hope.

The truth is that when something is important to you, you see to it that your child is educated and even coerced to follow through. He will brush his teeth because you won't tolerate any other option. If you give your child free rein on religion, what you are really saying is that religion is not very important to you. The message is being heard loud and clear.

Eleanor Roosevelt once said, "If you can give your children a trust in God, they will have one sure way of meeting all the uncertainties of existence." [2]

Unfortunately, most parents today fail to provide their children with this priceless foundation and opt for the "children choose" syndrome. It is to this type of mindset that the following story is directed.

Samuel Taylor Coleridge, the great English poet of the Romantic period, was once talking with a man who told him that he did not believe in giving children any religious instruction whatsoever. His theory was that the child's mind should not be prejudiced in any direction, but when he came to years of discretion, he should be permitted to choose his religious opinions for himself. Coleridge said nothing, but after a while he asked his visitor if he would like to see his garden. The man said he would, and Coleridge took him out into the garden, where only weeds were growing.

---

2. *The American Rabbi,* June 1993 page 46.

The man looked at Coleridge in surprise and said, "Why, this is not a garden! There are nothing but weeds here!"

"Well, you see" answered Coleridge, "I did not wish to infringe upon the liberty of the garden in any way. I was just giving the garden a chance to express itself and choose its own production."

Our psalmist was the victim of one of these types of abandonment. It was so traumatic, we see that it left him with a perpetual personality faultline. He has a weakness in his psyche that opens as soon as he is under stress. He is forever fearful, on some level, that he will be abandoned again. Yet in the end he is able to connect to his faith. It is deep and immutable. It is what enables him to reconnect with his emotional center. It is a faith best described by the following Chassidic tale.

There was a pair of disciples of a renowned Chassidic master who, every Passover, traveled long distances to spend the holiday in the court of their wise and learned teacher. One year, the owner of an inn where the two pious travelers had stopped to spend the night asked them to have their rabbi intercede with the Almighty to bless his childless marriage of fifteen years with a child. The disciples agreed to pass along this poignant request.

The next morning, the innkeeper's wife was seen parading about the streets with a magnificent new baby carriage. All her friends stopped to congratulate her, but she demurred, saying, "Not yet."

One year later, the disciples chose to again spend the night at that particular guesthouse en route to the rabbi's court. As it turned out, they were just in time to participate in the celebration of the innkeeper's newborn son's circumcision.

When they arrived at their rabbi's court the next day, one of the disciples requested a private audience. Sadly, he said: "Rebbi, you did not even know that innkeeper, yet your prayers for him were successful. I, on the other hand, have been your trusted disciple for many years and yet my wife and I remain without progeny after twenty years. Why have your prayers on our behalf remained unanswered?"

The Chassidic master looked at his disciple compassionately, clasped his hands, and asked him softly, "During all those years, did you ever buy a baby carriage?"[3]

Our psalmist lived his life with that level of faith. He was always buying the metaphoric baby carriage. It was that level of faith that kept him together in a life that had no end of pain and suffering.

He is a man haunted by enemies who want nothing more than to kill him. He was abandoned by his parents. Yet faith in God has sustained him through it all. That is the lesson of this psalm. In the end, even estrangement from parents and the accompanying emptiness and loneliness can be compensated for by a closeness that comes with a faith in God. Maybe it can even be the source to bring parents and their children back together again.

A brokenhearted father from the United States went to Israel. His only son had become a hippie who left college the year before and vanished without a trace.

Standing at the Wall in Jerusalem, the father wrote a prayer on a piece of paper, imploring God to restore his son to him unharmed. As he inserted his 'kvittel' (a paper with a petition to God written on it) in a crevice in the Wall, one of the many notes embedded there fell to the ground. He bent down to retrieve it and recognized a familiar handwriting. It was that of his lost son.

On the back of the paper was scrawled: "Dear God, please let me see my Mom and Dad again!"

The young man had also written his address on the note. And so there was a most joyous reunion because two people, father and son, had offered prayers at the Wall.

Look to the Lord;
be strong and of good courage!
O look to the Lord!

---

3. *Jewish Living,* April 1980.

— CHAPTER 24 —

Slander–Back at You

Four men of the cloth were having a confidential talk and discussing their vices.

"I like pork," the rabbi admitted.

"I drink a bottle of bourbon a day," said the Protestant minister.

"I have a girlfriend on the side," confessed the priest.

They all turned to the Baptist minister, who shrugged, "Me, I like to gossip."

I hesitated to open such an important and serious subject as this with a joke, but I think it expresses the concern and danger of gossip. (Besides, a good joke is a terrible thing to waste.) But gossip and malicious slander are so serious that the Talmud actually calls it a form of "triple murder."

When you kill a person, you actually kill a single soul, but when you gossip and slander, you are in one utterance destroying three.

The first victim is the one being gossiped about.

The second is the person who hears it and is polluted by it.

Finally and perhaps most surprising, the third is the one who says it.

After all, even the gossiper has a holy soul that should have elevated him. Instead, the gossiper actually sullies his soul and brings it down. It is the ultimate in negative efficiency! One act—three victims. And I do mean victims.

When on sabbatical, I received an e-mail story about a famous clothes designer who was said to have been a guest on Oprah. While on the show, the designer was purported to have made racist and anti-Semitic remarks. As the story went, it was so vulgar that Oprah dismissed her guest.

Readers of the e-mail were advised to show their disdain for his comments by boycotting the product line. (I have remained purposefully vague, as mentioning the name would only contribute to the sin.) After reading the forwarded message, I e-mailed the person who passed it on, asking for verification.

The story sounded suspect. Why would Oprah air it? Why had I not heard or read about it elsewhere than this anonymous e-mail? I could not get it verified, so I decided to ignore it. Sure enough, it was disclosed to be a hoax. Malicious, evil, and false as it was, how many became a party to it? How many passed it on and themselves became guilty of the slander?

What if it was a message about your father or mother and his or her company? What if it caused his business to fail? How many times has this happened on a small scale? How many lives have been ruined?

Hear my voice, O God, when I plead;
guard my life from the enemy's terror.
Hide me from a band of evil men,
from the crowd of evildoers,
who whet their tongues like swords;
they aim their arrows—cruel words—
to shoot from hiding at the blameless man;
they shoot him suddenly and without fear.
They encourage each other
to do evil matters;
they tell of laying hidden snares;
they ask "who could see them."
They devise false iniquities;
they have compelled a diligent search,
hiding their falsehood within themselves
and in the depth of their hearts.

Then God shot them with an arrow.
Suddenly they were wounded.
And they were made to stumble
by their own tongues;

all who saw them shook their heads.
And all men feared
and declared the work of God,
and His doing they understood.
The righteous will rejoice in God
and will take refuge in Him;
and all the upright in heart will glorify Him. (Ps. 64)

Gossip is one of the great social sins. Even more than robbery, which often but not always requires a fence to sell the stolen property, gossip cannot exist without another. Could Robinson Crusoe gossip before he discovered Friday?

How often have you heard a choice morsel of information that you so badly needed to tell that you felt like you were about to burst if you didn't get it out? What good is it to have the "scoop" on someone if you can't share it? Gossip requires a group, and that is the seed of its destructive power.

People always gossip with others, and somehow the group gives the seal of approval to the action. It is unstated but surely felt that if what I am saying is unacceptable, people wouldn't let me say it. The group reinforces and legitimizes the actions. Try to be in a group when someone is gossiping about another and say, "Enough. It is wrong to speak of another this way. I won't abide this belittlement of another human being."

First there are stares of disbelief, then the assumption that you are joking or putting them on. When they finally sense that you are serious, you can literally feel the chill descend on the group. It won't be long before you will sense the separation. You will feel apart without anyone having to move.

Perhaps someone will engage you in debate and tell you it's okay because it's true. They may look at you in disbelief and tell you not to be a nerd or whatever the term for outsider is in your group. The message will be clear and immediate.

"Get on the program and shut up, or leave the group and be

ready to be the next subject talked about." (Probably just after the door closes behind you.) Peer pressure is always with us, and at every stage in life it is hard to ignore.

Watch children in the playground or seniors around the pool in the condominium. Observe the mores of the "boys" at the country club or their wives on Fifth Avenue or Rodeo Drive.

But nothing touches the teenager for pressure to conform. Teenagers are never seen traveling in ones. Like weather maps that show the onset of a front, they are a line of triangles or half-circles attached somewhere, swooping in from one direction about to occupy and influence the happenings of the next area they invade.

Go to the mall. Try walking from point A to B without having to duck a phalanx of teenage girls marching in a straight, unbending line that would have made any Roman general proud. This is the ultimate breeding ground for gossip, slander, and purely malicious talk.

There is a whole genre of teen movies that are made from the point of view of an in-crowd, gossiping and constantly putting down everyone else. From the movie *Heathers* to *Pretty in Pink*, and *Carrie,* the theme is repeated over and over. There needs to be a group that sees itself as "cool" and nourishes itself on gossip and social ostracization of the individual.

This is what the psalmist was talking about when he said,

> *They encourage each other*
> *to do evil matters;*
> *they tell of laying hidden snares;*
> *they ask "who could see them."*
> *They devise false iniquities;*
> *they have compelled a diligent search,*
> *hiding their falsehood within themselves*
> *and in the depth of their hearts.*

I forever will remember and be influenced by a movie I saw as a young teenager. It was based on a play by the same name: *Tea and Sympathy*. It told of a sensitive young man in college who was constantly laughed at and whispered about. While everyone around him was into the macho sports and skirt-chasing scene, he was studious, sensitive, and socially inept. People hounded him unmercifully, including members of the faculty.

There was clearly an insinuation of homosexuality, though given the times and my own sheltered upbringing, I did not pick up on that until a much later reviewing. The gossip drives him into a state of self-doubt, depression, and even suicidal contemplation. He is saved in the end by the attention, support, and finally the kindly seduction of the wife of the faculty member who aided and abetted the rain of torment on him.

I'm not advocating adultery. I raise the scenario as a powerful example of the tyranny of a group, isolating someone and then feeding off them to satiate a communal need for bonding and false superiority.

There is another scenario of response and recompense. It is the proverbial "what comes around, goes around." Evil behavior will not go unpunished. Perhaps the words used by the slanderer will in the end be the words used about the slandered. Nevertheless, it sometimes might demand the intervention of forces beyond our control.

I am tempted to replay the end scene from the movie *Carrie* as the warning to all who gossip and slander. Beware your misdeeds—you never know how they will come back to haunt you in the end. Perhaps in the very words of your mouth, you lay the foundation for someone or something to turn it around on you.

As the psalmist so clearly implies,

They devise false iniquities;
they have compelled a diligent search,
hiding their falsehood within themselves
and in the depth of their hearts.
Then God shot them with an arrow.
Suddenly they were wounded.
And they were made to stumble
by their own tongues;
all who saw them shook their heads.

— CHAPTER 25 —

God, the Healer

Can you remember a time when you were so ill that you wondered what you had ever done to deserve such pain and suffering ? Have you or someone you know felt so miserable that you said something like "I wish I could die" or "Even death is starting to look good to me"?

Have you visited someone ill who was so depressed from their ailment that it was actually unbearable to be in their presence?

In Psalm 6 we meet someone like that who is suffering in a horrific way. He is in such physical and mental pain that he feels that death is coming if something doesn't change soon. And it is God whom he turns to, for that change to happen.

God, do not rebuke me with Your anger,
nor chastise me with Your rage.
Be gracious unto me, God,
for I am desolate;
heal me, God, for my bones are terrified.
My soul, too, is utterly terrified, and You, God—how long?
Return, God; free my soul;
deliver me as befits Your loving kindness.
For in death there is no mention of You;

in the lower world, who will acclaim You?
I am worn out with my sighing.
Every night I cause my bed to float;
I melt my couch in my tears.
My eye is dimmed from anger.
It has aged because of my tormentors.
Depart from me, all you evildoers,
for God has heard the voice of my weeping.
God has heard my supplication.
God will accept my prayer.
Ashamed and utterly terrified
will all my foes be.
They will return
and be instantaneously ashamed. (vs. 1-10)

Like many of us, he feels that his suffering is some form of punishment. He accepts that pain and suffering have their place in helping him learn and grow—but how much can he take?

God, do not rebuke me with Your anger,
nor chastise me with Your rage.

He is really hurting. His body hurts, and his soul is in turmoil. He is depressed and forlorn. Listen to the agony in his voice as he pleads with God for help.

Be gracious unto me, God,
for I am desolate;
heal me, God, for my bones are terrified.
My soul, too, is utterly terrified, and You, God—how long?

The pain and pathos are powerfully expressed. He feels that only God can give him the strength to heal, and yet nothing is happening. If anything, he is declining physically, and his spirits are crashing.

In a half-expressed thought, truncated perhaps by his own pain, he cries out more than speaks, and emits a call: "how long?" Can you see the pain on his face and feel the frustration in his heart? Can you feel the crushing burden of his anguish?

He has just enough energy to look up to God with his pleading eyes and emit a pathetic plea.

There's a pause—we don't know for how long—and he regains enough poise or energy to continue again. This time, though, he is more focused. He is ready to ask in a more direct way for help. He is going to make his case.

> *Return, God; free my soul;*
> *deliver me as befits Your loving kindness.*

Now we are about to see that death has crossed his mind, for he projects ahead to it as a possibility. He says to God,

> *For in death there is no mention of You;*
> *in the lower world, who will acclaim You?*

He now returns to describing his predicament. He is so depressed he has no energy to do anything for himself. He is immobile and deteriorating rapidly.

> *I am worn out with my sighing.*
> *Every night I cause my bed to float;*
> *I melt my couch in my tears.*
> *My eye is dimmed from anger.*
> *It has aged because of my tormentors.*

And then it all changes.

Somehow he feels he has been heard, and that alone starts him on his recovery. His energy is back. His depression is replaced with assertiveness. He is well. God and he are together again. God has inspired him, reinvigorated his spirit, and his body has followed suit. The world that gathered in joy at his decline is now banished in shame. He has his God, and through Him, a healed soul and body—let no one stand in his way.

> *Depart from me, all you evildoers,*
> *for God has heard the voice of my weeping.*
> *God has heard my supplication.*
> *God will accept my prayer.*

Ashamed and utterly terrified
will all my foes be.
They will return
and be instantaneously ashamed.

It's a powerful psalm, but is it real? Is there a connection between the soul and the body? Can one really be sick of body and find healing from belief in and prayer to God?

Perhaps the better question may be, Is there a religion that doesn't believe there is a connection between spiritual wholeness and physical well-being?

The Talmud states (Nedarim 41a) that a person does not recover from his illness until all of his sins are forgiven.

Indeed, in the Bible we see cases of illness such as the leprosy of Miriam, which derives directly from her sin of slander. Even if we see this metaphorically rather than literally, we understand that our proper moral behavior reinforces our wellness, whereas our moral degeneracy leads us to sickness and decay.

Franz Alexander, known as the father of psychosomatic medicine, wrote more than half a century ago that "there is much evidence that, just as certain pathological microorganisms have a specific affinity for certain organs, so also certain emotional conflicts possess specificities and accordingly tend to afflict certain internal organs." (*Love, Medicine, and Miracles,* p. 90)

There are what Dr. Bernie Siegel calls target organs, in which certain psychological factors cause a specific organ to become the focus of disease. He tells of a man named Lee who had a persistent hoarseness that was eventually diagnosed as carcinoma of the larynx. The man was a nonsmoker, and the location of the tumor was therefore quite unusual. Being sensitive to the issue of body and soul, Lee realized there were psychological factors involved. Together he and Dr. Siegel probed his background for the significance.

The man's family was large and noisy, and often when the boy was talking loudly, his father put his hand around his throat and squeezed, telling him, "Shut up. Shut up Lee," in a husky, whispery voice, just like Lee's later esophageal speech.

Dr. Siegel explains, "Lee's case is not unusual. Target organs—parts of the body with special significance to the conflicts or losses in a person's life—are the most likely areas for disease to take root." (p. 90) How far of a jump is it to sinful behavior leading to bodily disease, or spiritual growth leading to bodily cure?

Dr. Siegel doesn't wait until near-death to bring God into the picture, as other physicians do. He connects with the patient's spirituality right from the beginning, when it can be most helpful. "After all," he argues, "a person who believes in a benevolent higher power" has a potent reason for hope, and hope is physiologic."

The curing is the patient's responsibility, not God's, but a believer has the mindset to do the work. Dr Siegel encourages his patients to have faith in God but not to expect Him to do all the work. Most potently, he states that patients not think of illness being God's will, but rather our deviation from God's will.

Our emotional state is crucial to our well-being. When we are happy, when our soul is at peace, we tend to be of strong body. Those who are at peace with themselves and their world have fewer problems and fewer illnesses.

Our psalmist is not at peace. He knows he's done wrong and is being punished, and for a while he sinks into depression. From there, his suffering and illness increase. He is in a negative spiral, a vicious cycle that will consume him if he can not find a way out. The depression is what is now keeping him back. Indeed, it is now the main source of his pain and affliction. If he doesn't break loose, he will surely die.[1]

Our psalmist reaches out beyond himself to get out of his depression. He reaches to his faith in God's goodness and His presence to take him out of his negativity and depression. God will give him the strength to rise from the morass of sadness and negativity to a view of optimism and hope.

Here is a similar story of an external force helping a woman break out of a self-destructive pattern and heal herself.

---

1. Depressed men are twice as likely to get cancer as nondepressives. A study of identical twins, one of whom in each pair had leukemia, showed that the one with the disease had become severely depressed or suffered an emotional loss beforehand, while the other, healthy twin had not (Siegel, p. 78).

A woman named Denise, a breast cancer patient, wrote the following letter to Dr. Siegel in which she told of a visit to a faith healer in Worcester, Massachusetts:

> After his sermon, he said that each one would know in their heart if they were the one to be called. He turned around to his audience of over 1500 people and said, "I have a strong experience with someone concerning a rose. She has a disease in her chest area."
>
> I felt my insides move as I recalled the night before while I was at dinner, when I took a fresh rose out of the vase on our table, and smelled it. Someone had told me I had to take time to smell the flowers of life. However, I didn't stand up. I thought it couldn't be me.
>
> The healer then approached a woman who had stood up. Her name was Rose, and she had breast cancer. He blessed her but said, "You are not the one I am experiencing."
>
> He said, "She also has breast cancer, and is wearing a beige top."
>
> That morning I had put on a pair of black slacks and a long-sleeved black blouse. Then I decided to put on my short-sleeved beige blouse as an overlay, felt too fat, and took it off, and then decided to put it back on again.
>
> At this point I stood up, and he called me down to the front of the audience. He asked me about my illness, and as I stood there full of tears and emotions, I shall never forget how his face looked. He didn't have any eyes, just dark pools of infinity. As he anointed my forehead, he said, "'You have to let go of your anguish."
>
> And with this, I experienced a bolt of energy that passed through my body. I felt a scream come from my mouth, and I fell toward the floor into the arms of the ushers behind me.

This experience was a turning point for Denise, She began to be able to set priorities for herself and make choices based on her own needs. She used psychotherapy and chemotherapy, ended a relationship that she felt was damaging to her, and sold her business, which had been a major source of stress. Finally allowing herself to express a lifetime of pent-up anger, frustration, and sadness, she cried for days and found that for the first time she was able to accept the child within her.

At the end of her letter, she wrote, "This was the first time I had ever given myself the privilege and dignity to mourn my own pains and agonies. Now that all the debris has moved from my soul, my [inner] child and I are one. I feel total integration, self love, and forgiveness. I need never judge others, for I no longer need to judge myself."

Spirituality, unconditional love, and the ability to see that pain and problems are opportunities for growth and redirection—these things allow us to make the best of the time we have. Then we realize that the present moment is all we have, but it is infinite. We see that there is no real past or future, and that as soon as we start thinking in terms of past and future—regretting and wishing—we lose ourselves in judgmental thinking. In one of the countries where people regularly live to be a hundred, people have a saying: "Yesterday is gone, tomorrow isn't here yet, so what is there to worry about?"

How we see the world around us and our place in it affects the totality of our being. When we have hope (and a belief in God gives hope), we can grab control of even a death sentence and reduce the severity and sometimes even eliminate the decree itself.

There's a truly inspiring story that illustrates the point.

Exceptional patients have the ability to throw statistics aside—to say, "I can be a survivor"—even when the doctor isn't wise enough to do so. Just think of the courage it took for someone to conquer a certain type of cancer that no one had ever conquered before. Hope instilled that kind of courage in William Calderon, who achieved the first documented recovery from Acquired Immune Deficiency Syndrome (AIDS). Calderon was diagnosed in December 1982. His doctors told him he would probably be dead in six months. Understandably, he became depressed and hopeless. Almost immediately Kaposi's sarcoma, the type of cancer that most often accompanies AIDS, appeared and began spreading rapidly on all areas of his skin and throughout his gastrointestinal tract.

Soon Judith Skutch, co-founder with astronaut Edgar

Mitchell of the Institute of Noetic Sciences and now President of the Foundation for Inner Peace, arrived at Calderon's hair-styling salon for her regular appointment. Noticing by his eyes that he had been weeping, she got him to tell her the reason.

Her next words turned out to be the key to saving his life. She said, "William, you don't have to die. You can get well."

Skutch described the Simontons' work with cancer patients. With unwavering love and support from her and from his lover, Calderon came to believe in his own survival. By continuing at the job he loved, he refused to give in to the disease. Instead he began meditating and using mental imagery to combat it. He worked to restore strained relationships with his family and achieved peace of mind by forgiving people he felt had hurt him. He loved his body with exercise, good nutrition, and vitamin supplements. And from that point on, his immune system showed increased response and his tumors began to shrink. Two years after the diagnosis, Calderon showed no signs of AIDS. (Siegel, *Love, Medicine and Miracles,* p. 40)

Dr. Granger Westberg, founder of many wholistic centers believes that half to three-quarters of all illnesses originate in problems of the spirit, rather than breakdowns of the body. The physical symptoms are often only the "tickets of admission" to a process of self-discovery and spiritual change. To begin that true healing, each of us must make the leap of faith described in a poem by Apollinaire.

> Come to the edge.
> No, we will fall.
>
> Come to the edge.
> No, we will fall.
>
> They came to the edge.
> He pushed them, and they flew.

Our psalmist was drowning in anger and depression. His soul was crushed, and he had no way out of his misery except to believe in God and be inspired to fly to Him. He called out,

Return, God; free my soul;
deliver me as befits your loving kindness.

He suffered through the hard times, but he grew and developed and came through the other side, healed and whole

Depart from me, all you evildoers,
for God has heard the voice of my weeping.
God has heard my supplication.
God will accept my prayer.

And he did.

CHAPTER 26

Free My Soul

There is a famous expression we are all familiar with. We often hear people say "out of the mouth of babes."

Usually we are impressed by the simplicity, appropriateness, and innocence of the child's comments. I have begun to wonder if it is the innocence of babes that opens our eyes to the wonders of the universe—or is it the unnecessary sophistication of adults that blocks or obscures our view? The following appeared in the *Los Angeles Times*.

"Listen to this, said my friend Nancy, calling from Michigan. Its the greatest story!"

And was it ever, one that went straight to the heart of a mother-to-be. It concerned a couple known by a friend of a friend of Nancy's. The couple had just become parents for the second time, and shortly after they brought their new addition home from the hospital, their first child, a three-year-old, began making a curious demand.

"I really need to talk to the baby," said the firstborn. "I need to talk to the baby alone."

The parents were reluctant to leave the kids by themselves, but the child persisted, and after some months, they relented.

They left the children in the baby's room and turned on the baby monitor before they walked out. Then they waited.

After a moment, the toddler spoke: "Hurry up and tell me what God looks like," he whispered urgently to the baby. "I'm starting to forget."

Rabbi David Wolpe, who wrote an important book on God, said the following to a reporter, which was subsequently printed in the paper.

He wrote,

> Over a year ago I spoke to a large group of children in Dallas. I asked them, "What would your mother say if you asked her what she thought about God?"
>
> A girl in the very first row jumped to her feet and waved her hand. Her answer was brief and memorable, "She would say—ask your father!"
>
> When the laughter died down, I thought about the sad truth of that answer. Many Jews are afraid to open the conversation. Too many Jewish children grow up hearing their parents' views on everything from health-care reform to foreign aid, but never discussing God.

Children have no problem with the concept of God. It's their parents who've become too sophisticated. God becomes detached, distanced, allegorized, metaphorized, anything but taken seriously.

A father came home from work. As always, his daughter came running to him and kissed him. She continued to shower him with kisses even as he turned his face away from her.

The father said, "Look at what you are doing. You are wasting so many kisses on empty air.

In utter simplicity, the child looked up at her father and said, "But Dad, God is everywhere. I am not wasting these kisses. I am kissing God."

Our psalmist understood the need for God.

A psalm of David,
when he was in the wilderness of Judah;

God, You are my Almighty;
I will seek You;
my soul thirsts for You;
my flesh longs for You,
in a dry and weary land without water.
Thus in the sanctuary have I perceived You,
To see our might and glory.
For better is Your kindness than life;
my lips will praise You.
So I will bless You throughout my life;
in Your name will I lift my hands. (Ps. 63, vs. 1-5)

When he was in the desert away from the temple, he recognized his need for God. It was as powerful as any biological drive. The need equaled the thirst for water in the arid desert. He knows what he is talking about. He has experienced the euphoria of being near God. He remembers from his former days in the tabernacle how exhilarating it was to be near God . With that knowledge, he is not prepared to exist without Him. He longs for the opportunity to praise and worship God.

Something is going on here! This psalm is so unlike the others. He wants to reach out his hands in a gesture of prayer, to uplift his hands in devotion to God. There is a great craving, a yearning for something even more than usual. The clue to it all, I believe, comes from the next few verses.

As with fat and marrow,
my soul will be satisfied,
and with joyous language
will my mouth give praise.
When I remember You upon my couch,
in the night watches I meditate upon You.
For You have been a help to me,
and in the shadow of Your wings
I will joyfully sing.
My soul is attached to You;
Your right hand supports me.
But those who seek destruction for my soul,
they will enter into the abyss of the earth. (vs. 6-10)

What he really wants is to achieve the mystical connection of his soul with the highest level, the very source of its creation—God. This, in the end, is the spiritual quest of all mystics in all religions. The language may change, the terminology and cosmic metaphor may vary, but the yearning for union and oneness is universal.

We each have a soul. It comes from God and returns to God. While it is in our body, it is in exile from its lofty source. Like all of us who are far from home, it longs for any opportunity to connect with its spiritual abode.

Sometimes when we have departed home, we can return for a visit. Failing that, even a telephone call or an e-mail is something that we would crave. Young campers wait in their bunks as the mail is distributed and pray for a letter from home. Soldiers separated from loved ones by war pine for any connection to home.

So, too, the soul wishes to connect back to the lofty, heavenly source of its origin. While we are alive, the soul is in us, not in the spiritual realm. It is here for a purpose and must endure the limitations of the physical world, but it longs for some contact with home. It wants spiritual nourishment from the heavenly table, no less than the body craves its daily caloric intake.

As with fat and marrow,
my soul will be satisfied,

This is what the psalmist is blessed to be able to give to his soul. His prayers and his meditations open a channel for his soul to at least visit the celestial realm. For a few brief moments, the soul nearly departs the body as it connects closer and closer to its heavenly home.

and with joyous language
will my mouth give praise.
When I remember You upon my couch,
in the night watches I meditate upon You.
For You have been a help to me,
and in the shadow of Your wings
I will joyfully sing.

This is what the psalmist is talking about. He remembers the overwhelmingly blissful moments when, in meditation, his soul made contact with the divine source. The euphoria of the first part of the psalm, and the continued craving for more, comes from this connection. Indeed, he alludes to having soared to the highest levels, to having actually connected with some aspect of God.

My soul is attached to You;
Your right hand supports me.

For the spiritually attuned person, this is what prayer and meditation provide. Prayer reminds us not of our limitations, but of our unending potentiality. Prayer takes us to places that we otherwise would never inhabit. Prayer brings us closer to the source of help and of hope.

Therefore the soul, and we, as hosts, rejoice in the opportunity to pray and connect to God.

and in the shadow of Your wings
I will joyfully sing.
My soul is attached to You;
Your right hand supports me.

— CHAPTER 27 —

Immortality

If there is a category of people more spoiled and more self-possessed than the young, it can only be the rich. This is best seen in the following story.

An elderly lady was driving a big, new expensive car and was preparing to back into a parallel parking space. Suddenly, a young man in a small sports car zoomed into the space, beating her out of it.

The lady charged out of her car. She demanded to know why he had done that, when he could easily tell she was trying to park there and had been there first.

His response was simply, "Because I'm young and I'm quick."

When he came back out a few minutes later, he found the elderly lady using her big new car as a battering ram. She was backing up and then ramming it into his parked car.

Now he was very angry and asked her why she was wrecking his car.

Her response was simply, "Because I'm old and I'm rich."

The rich have always fascinated us. Throughout time, people have told stories of the rich and powerful, princes and noblemen.

We read of princesses and their gowns, their jewelry, and

their court life. Shakespeare would not bother with regular people when he had royalty and noblemen to play with.

In our day, the TV tabloids deal with the wealthy and the famous, film stars and the très chic. More people can identify Donald Trump and tell you his life story then can recognize the prime minister of Canada or the heads of state of NATO countries.

This fascination with the wealthy is not limited to the poor looking in from the outside. The rich are totally enamored with themselves and feel they have a special entitlement.

I was talking with a man who manufactures and sells beautiful silverware. His items cost from hundreds to thousands of dollars. He shocked me when he said that he prefers middle- and upper-middle-class buyers to the very rich. He said they were easier to deal with.

He told me of a very wealthy man coming into the store. He wanted to buy an item for thousands of dollars. The wealthy man insisted on buying it at a ridiculously low price. The storekeeper told him the cost and in negotiation gave him the best offer he could. The wealthy buyer refused to accept it. He somehow felt that because he was terribly wealthy, he should get it for next to nothing. When his arguments got nowhere, he threatened to walk.

He challenged the owner, certain this merchant wasn't going to let this large deal walk. The shop owner told him he wasn't in business to lose money, and in the end he asked the man to leave.

He told me he could not believe the arrogance of this man, who truly believed he should get the item for next to nothing just because he was wealthy. The wealthy often believe that there are two sets of rules in the world, one for the rich and one for the poor.

In fact, they believe there are two sets of rules for the "other" world, as well. If you can buy anything you want here in this world and you feel that everything is coming to you, why not the world to come? Why not be able to buy your ticket to heaven? Why can't immortality be purchased?

In his book *The Gift of Life,* Rabbi Samuel Chiel tells of William Robinowitz of Washington, D.C., who donated $10,000 to his synagogue. (The story is from many years ago, when $10,000 was a huge sum of money.) For this the main entrance to the synagogue was to be called "the Robinowitz Foyer."

Later the officers decided to add a plaque to the foyer with additional names. Mr. Robinowitz sued the the congregation, claiming that he had been promised that no other names would ever be hung in the foyer and that it would be reserved for him as a "perpetual and permanent memorial."

In his suit before the U.S. district court, he argued that to hang other names on the foyer would destroy the purpose of his "exclusive" memorial.[1]

That's not what God had in mind, according to the psalmist.

In time of trouble, why should I fear
the encompassing evil of those who would supplant me—
men who trust in their riches,
who glory in their great wealth?
Ah, it cannot redeem a man,
or pay his ransom to God; (Ps. 49, vs. 6-8)

So many people believe that they can buy their way out of a tough situation. Look at donations in charity boxes whenever there is a crisis. To many, there is a sense that God can be bought off. No matter the crisis, if we make a pledge, give a contribution, or build a new wing, we can buy off the evil decree. This concept is widespread and totaly ludicrous, as the following story illustrates.

A young clergyman was flying from New York to Los Angeles. They were 20,000 feet over the Rocky Mountains when, without warning, one of the engines fell off.

The pilot, struggling with the controls, managed to bring the plane back to an even keel, then asked the stewardess if the passengers were overly nervous.

"They're near the point of panic," she told him. The pilot turned the controls over to the co-pilot and went back to where the clergyman was sitting.

---

1. *The Gift of Life,* by Rabbi Samuel Chiel, p. 147, 148.

"The rest of the passengers are alarmed," he said urgently. "Do something religious."

So the clergyman took up a collection.

It doesn't work that way. As the psalmist continues,

the price of life is too high;
and so one ceases to be, forever.
Shall he live eternally,
and never see the grave? (vs. 9-10)

What comeback could there be to an argument as final as death? Yet never underestimate the will or ingenuity of the wealthy, when it comes to challenging the egalitarian finality of mortality.

I knew of a wealthy man who decided that death was neither inevitable nor irreversible. He became involved with a cryogenic organization and spent a lot of money preparing to put his body into deep freeze as soon as he died. The theory was that if they could preserve his body intact, then later when they discovered a cure for whatever disease he died from, he would be revived and cured. A latter-day Dr. Frankenstein.

We used to joke, cruelly perhaps, that if you were with him at a social gathering and he were to suddenly die, you should dunk his head in ice water and call for the "ice man."

But death really is the great equalizer.

For one sees that the wise die,
that the foolish and the arrogant both perish.
Leaving their wealth to others.
Their grave is their eternal home,
the dwelling place for all generations
of those once famous on earth.
Man does not abide in honor;
he is like the beasts that perish. (vs. 11-13)

If the rich don't get it, their children are even more removed from reality. They have the capacity to see their parents pass away and to somehow disassociate the finality of the passing from their own finite mortality. They convince themselves that their money and largesse will somehow buy them immortality here on earth. They do this because their focus is on the world of the material, the world of the present and of things.

> *This is their way—*
> *their folly remains with them,*
> *and their descendants*
> *take pleasure in their speech, Selah.* (vs. 14)

This explains large monuments that the rich build for themselves. From the pyramids of ancient Egypt to the large and ornate mausoleums we see at cemeteries, the wealthy assume they'll be remembered in direct proportion to the size of the monument they build or leave behind.

The famous showman Billy Rose died on February 10, 1966, but it took months to inter his body. His sisters fought with the executor of the estate because they wanted to spend a great deal of money on his burial, which they believed was his due. After sixteen months, a compromise was reached. The mausoleum at the cemetery would cost $60,000 (in 1966 dollars!). The plot, large enough for eighty graves, was $45,000. Perpetual care was $19,000, coming to a total of $124,000.[2]

Of this type of folly the psalmist knew only too well. He wrote,

> *Like sheep—they are destined for the grave;*
> *death shall be their shepherd.*
> *And the upright shall dominate them*
> *at morning;*
> *their form will be consumed in the grave;*
> *(it will not remain) their dwelling place.* (vs. 15)

There is no answer to death in the ostentatious display of wealth and property. Not here in the present, nor in the future. Certainly not in the real immortality that is God's gift of existence in the world to come.

---

2. *The Gift of Life*, by Rabbi Samuel Chiel, p. 147, 148.

We too often focus on the differences in religion. There is a need between groups to prove their superiority. So many groups feel a compulsion to proselytize, to show how another view must be wrong because there is only one truth, and they have it.

We become so obsessed with being right, with having the one true religion, that we fail to realize that there can be many truths for the different people of the world. The proof of this position comes not from focusing on our differences, but on the similarities. The packaging may differ, the filter through which we see the world may vary, but for most of us it is the same world, the same God, and the same principle.

Is there a major religion in the world that doesn't teach the eternity of the soul? Do Christian martyrs' souls not ascend to heaven for their martyrdom? Are Moslems who die in Jihad not guaranteed to ascend to a heavenly abode? Do not Jews believe that to die for the sanctification of God's name is a mitzvah (commandment) that will surely be rewarded in the world to come?

From Native American religions, which talk of the spirits of the ancestors, to the Buddhists and their belief in reincarnation, the idea of reward and punishment in the spiritual world is universal.

That is what the psalmist understands that real immortality is all about. He is not bothered by the seeming success of the wealthy. He knows in the end that what he does, who he is, and how he conducts himself will earn him the only lasting eternity. His soul will be with God.

But God will redeem my soul
from the (grasp of) the grave,
for He will take me to Himself, Selah. (vs. 16)

He goes on to repeat and to reiterate,

Fear not when a man grows rich,
when the glory of his house is increased.
For when he dies,
he shall carry nothing away,
his glory will not descend after him.
Because while he lived, he blessed his soul,

(saying), they will praise you
because you have done well for yourself. (vs. 17-19)

The psalmist points out again how the rich never get it. They are deluded by their wealth into thinking they have it all, when in the end they have nothing.

Imagine you were given a choice. You could be rich, eat steak every night for seventy years, enjoy it and have no weight or cholesterol problems, and then have nothing.

Or you could be poor, eat breadcrumbs and spoiled food for those same seventy years, and then for eternity eat steak and enjoy it. Which would you choose?

In the long run, who is the poor and who is the rich man?

The rich never get it !

There was a debate between a philosopher and a cynic on this very point. Which is more important: money or wisdom?

"Wisdom" says the philosopher.

"Ha!" scoffs the cynic. "If wisdom is more important than money, why is it that the wise wait on the rich, and not the rich on the wise?"

"Because," says the scholar, "the wise, being wise, understand the value of money; but the rich, being only rich, do not know the value of wisdom."

This same idea is seen in the following very real story that could be about a minister or priest just as easily as it is about a Rabbi.

A rabbi was criticized by his leadership for spending too much time with the richest members of the congregation. In his defense he responded, "You don't understand. It takes very little time to convince the poor people of the synagogue they are poor. It just takes longer with the wealthy ones, to convince them they are also poor." (Michael Zedek, *The American Rabbi*, Spring 1996, p.46)

He will join the generation of his fathers;
they shall not see light, for all eternity.
Man with all his splendor,
(but) without understanding,
is likened to the silenced animals. (vs. 20-21)

Wealth can be a blessing, but it too easily degenerates into a smugness that perverts one's perspective. Too many fall into the trap without even realizing it. Indeed, the truly wise must work hard to protect themselves from the corruptive arrogance of wealth.

A story is told about Rabbi Akiva. He took a trip to the market one day to sell a pearl that he had saved. As he arrived, he was greeted by a very wealthy man who chose to appear as a pauper in public. He wore degrading clothing and chose to sit with the poor in the synagogue.

When this disguised wealthy man saw the pearl that Rabbi Akiva held, he wanted to buy it. He persuaded Rabbi Akiva to accompany him to his home, where he would pay its value. When the two reached the home of the wealthy man, Rabbi Akiva was surprised to be greeted by the servants of this poorly dressed man. They tended to all the needs of the two men and placed their master on his golden chair. The wealthy man then ordered his servants to bring him money to pay Rabbi Akiva for the pearl.

Following this exchange, Rabbi Akiva was invited to dinner. After finishing the meal, Rabbi Akiva asked, "After the Lord has granted you all this great wealth, why do you degrade yourself so much and sit with the unfortunate poor?"

The wealthy man answered, "Rabbi, the psalm says, 'Man is like vapor; his days are like a passing shadow.' Money doesn't last forever. Therefore I think it does me a lot of good to sit with the poor. My spirit will not become arrogant and I will not become haughty because of my great wealth."

Money can be very deceiving at times. It can blur our vision with little difficulty. This man knew that in spite of his great wealth, he was no equal to his Creator.[3]

There is a place of compromise in the struggle between immortality in this world, which is so elusive, and the immortality of the spiritual world to come. I believe that there is a way to leave a mark here that will cause us to be remembered long after we are gone. It may even earn us a better place in the world to come.

---

3. Rabbi Stefan Weinberg, The Rabbinical Assembly Homiletics Service, 187.

In his remarkable and moving handbook on grief and mourning, Rabbi William Silverman relates the following story:

There was a young man named David Levy whose sole ambition from an early age was to be immortalized in human history. How this man wanted his name to be known!

When he was a youngster, David Levy carved his name on a tree in the woods and he thought, *Now everybody who goes by this tree will know David Levy.*

His family moved away, and years later when he came back and went to the tree, he discovered that it had been chopped down. His name was gone.

He then decided to chisel his name into a rock perched on top of a cliff.

When he came back again many years later, he discovered that the rain and elements had eroded the letters. His name could no longer be deciphered.

In time, he became a successful businessman and he declared, "I will erect an imposing building and I will call it 'The David Levy Building.'"

So he did, but some years later, a fire burned the structure to the ground.

Discouraged and despairing of ever perpetuating his name, he began to share his means with worthy causes and needy people.

One day he went to the ward of a children's hospital and brought toys for the poor children.

One little girl looked up with gratitude in her eyes and said, "Mr. Levy, I will never forget you."

He smiled as he answered, "Thank you, dear. That is sweet of you to say, but I'm afraid that after a while, you will."

"Oh, no," the child responded. "I will never forget you, because, you see, your name is written upon my heart."[4]

The classic and lasting form of immortality will always be the reward the soul receives as a consequence of the body's behavior. It is between us and God and will never be seen in this corporeal existence. We can't take anything with us when we leave,

---

4. David J. Meyer, *American Rabbi*, April 1995, p.47-48.

but we can leave behind something that will last and give us a quasiphysical immortality.

Martin Buxbaum wrote,

> You can use most any measure
> When you're speaking of success
> You can measure it in fancy home,
> Expensive car or dress.
> But the measure of your real success
> Is the one you cannot spend.
> It's the way your kids describe you
> When they're talking to a friend.[5]

Would that our children and children's children be a living memorial for us all.

---

5. "Dear Abby," April 14, 1994.

— CHAPTER 28 —

Sibling Rivalry–
Exception or Norm?

Behold, how good and how pleasant it is
when brothers also dwell together in unity.
Like the precious oil upon the head
running down onto the beard,
the beard of Aaron
that comes down
upon the edge of his garments;
like the dew of Mount Hermon
that comes down upon the mountains of Zion;
from there God commanded the blessing
of everlasting life. (Ps. 133)

This is a short but extremely intriguing psalm. It seems at first glance to have no continuity. It starts out talking about brotherly unity and ends up with eternal life. The middle seems to have no connection to either part.

I read this psalm over and over again. I was attracted to the first line. It may be because in Hebrew this line was one of the first Hebrew songs I ever learned. It was the first song I ever sang in the round. In my circle, growing up, it was as common as "Michael, row the boat ashore, Hallelujah." We even sang it around the campfire in a similar manner. To me the power and the message of this psalm were included in the opening line.

Behold, how good and how pleasant it is
when brothers also dwell together in unity.

The rest of the psalm didn't fit until I realized that the remainder of the psalm really elaborated on and developed this one concept. The unity of brothers was as pleasant and perhaps as significant as the blessings of eternal life. Maybe it is as rare and esoteric, as well.

A Sunday school teacher was teaching the importance of love in the home. She illustrated her point by referring to the commandment "Honor thy father and thy mother." Then she asked if there was a commandment that taught how to treat sisters and brothers. One little boy from a large family raised his hand quickly. Innocently he asked, "Thou shalt not kill?"

Much has been written about sibling rivalry. How is it that children of the same parents, the same genes and upbringing, could historically have so much animosity? What happened to "Blood is thicker than water" and other such sayings that assume the family bond? I wonder if family unity is only a saying and family quarrels, the norm?

Look at the first book of the Bible, Genesis. Are the brothers allies, or foes? Cain and Abel are the first two brothers ever to exist. Cain kills Abel. Cain thus introduces and enters sibling rivalry into the "big leagues."

Abraham has to abandon his family to develop his religious destiny. His son Isaac can only flourish after the banishing of his half-brother, Ishmael. Isaac's twin sons, Jacob and Esau, are prenatal rivals, fighting in the womb. The entire record of their interaction is confrontational and seems always to totter on the brink of murder. Jacob has twelve sons, one of whom is almost murdered by his brother. In the end he is "only" sold by them into slavery.

Perhaps the lesson of Genesis is that sibling rivalry comes easily and naturally.

I read of two brothers who sat the entire day on Yom Kippur, the holiest day of the Jewish year, in the front row, on separate sides of the sanctuary. It was well known that for forty years they had not talked to each other. Once one brother was asked, "What was the argument all about?"

He replied, "I really don't remember. It happened many years ago, but I am still deeply hurt!"

Perhaps the years of competing for parental affection causes the jealousy. Maybe siblings' realization that they are competing for limited parental resources causes tension. When siblings understand, for instance, that the inheritance to be left to the children will not be distributed in an equal way, resentment develops.

In the ancient world, the first-born received the majority of the inheritance and the family power. Is it merely a coincidence that in every generation, an ongoing rivalry took place between brothers in a family where all who led were not first-born? Neither Abraham nor Isaac, Jacob nor Joseph were first-born. The source of the tensions seems obvious.

The gap between the goal and the reality is often significant. Cultures, religions, and societies sometimes develop standards that reflect not the actual norm but a wish, a goal that they hope will be reached.

The cases of fulfillment become the inspirational tales to guide and motivate the population not to what comes easily, but to what should be.

To have familial unity is difficult and rare. Therefore it is as sweet when it happens, as the blessing of eternal life.

Here are some classic and modern tales that inspire us to what could be.

The first tale speaks to the fantasy level I talked about above. It is a classic tale that expresses the highest level of brotherly love.

There is an ancient legend about the two brothers, one rich and the other poor.

One night, the rich brother could not sleep. He said to himself, "I'm rich, but I'm single. I need so little. My brother is poor. He has a wife and children. He needs so much more than I do."

He rose from his bed in the middle of the night, went to his storehouse, filled two large baskets with grain, and started for his brother's home.

By coincidence, the poor brother could not sleep, either. "It's true that I am poor and my brother is rich," he said, "but I have children. When I grow old, they will care for me. My brother has no family; he is all alone. Who will care for him in his old age? He needs more than I." So he, too, rose and went to his meager storehouse, filled a small basket with grain, and started for his brother's home.

As they walked in the stillness of the night, by the light of the moon, they met. Each looked at the other, and each understood what was in the other's heart. They embraced; they kissed and wept, and then a heavenly voice was heard saying, "This ground sanctified by the tears of brotherly love, will be the place where My house shall be built," and according to Jewish tradition, when King Solomon built the Temple in Jerusalem, it was on this spot that it was erected.

The tale is touching.

Unfortunately, the fact that the temple was built here, as a testimony to this love, is an indication to how special and rare this kind of love really is.

The more common love that emerges from the rivalry for parents' affection and resources is powerfully expressed in the following letter to Ann Landers.

> Dear Ann Landers: Your column on reconciliation day changed my life. But let me start from the beginning. My brother and I were born 20 months apart. Mom dressed us alike and many thought we were twins. Tommy was better at basketball but I was better at soccer. He played a great trombone and I was pretty good on the drums. I was lousy in English and he did my homework. He wasn't so hot in math, so I helped him out. We were competitive but there were never any serious fights or arguments . . . It was always understood that my brother and I would go into the family business started by our grandfather. We knew something about it, having worked there most summers since we were teenagers. Tommy, being older, went in first. I decided to take a year off after college and travel. While I was in South Africa, Dad died suddenly of a heart attack. When I came home for the funeral, I got the shock of my life. He did not have a will. Mom inher-

ited everything. She was fond of Tom's wife and didn't care much for mine. So the long and short of it was that I was out of luck. My wife and I decided to move out of town, borrow some money from her father, and start our own business. We cut all family ties. Ten years passed. Mom died. We did not go to her funeral. I was angry and bitter, having felt that I had been cheated. Two weeks ago I received a copy of your column on reconciliation from Tommy. Across the top, he had written, "I miss you. Please call me." That very evening I called and we both cried. The following weekend, he and his wife and their two kids came to see us. It was my birthday. That was the greatest gift that I have ever received in my life."

In a world of fluctuation, the brothers rediscovered the comforting steadfastness of family love. The spirit of family. Or in the words of our psalmist,

Behold, how good and how pleasant it is
when brothers also dwell together in unity.

The following is one of the most powerful stories I have ever read about what it means to be a caring and loving brother. It is to me the very embodiment of the psalmist's elevation of brotherly unity to the level of everlasting life.

The author, Ray Angell, tells of a college friend named Paul, who received a new automobile from his brother as a present. When Paul came out of his office, a street kid was walking around the shiny new car, admiring it. "Is this your car, mister?" he asked.

Paul nodded. "My brother gave it to me."

The boy looked astounded. "You mean your brother gave it to you, and it didn't cost you nothing? Boy, I wish. . ."

He hesitated, and Paul knew what he was going to wish. He was going to wish that he had a brother like that.

But what the lad said jarred Paul all the way down to his heels. "I wish," the boy went on, "that I could be a brother like that."

Paul looked at the boy in astonishment, then impulsively asked, "Would you like to take a ride?"

"Oh, yes! I'd love that!"

After a short while, the boy turned and with eyes aglow said, "Mister, would you mind driving in front of my house?" Paul smiled a little. He thought he knew what the lad wanted—to show his neighbors that he could ride in a big automobile. But Paul was wrong.

"Will you stop right there where those two steps are?" the boy asked.

He ran up the steps. Then, in a little while, Paul heard him coming back, but not quite so fast.

He was carrying his little crippled brother. He sat him down on the bottom step, then sort of squeezed up against him and pointed to the car.

"There she is, buddy, just like I told you upstairs. His brother gave it to him, and it didn't cost a him cent. And someday I'm gonna give you one just like it. Then you can see for yourself all the pretty things that I've been trying to tell you about."

Paul got out and lifted the little lad to the front seat of his car. The shining-eyed older brother climbed in beside him and the three of them began a very memorable ride. (From *Making Miracles Happen,* by Michael Zedeck.)

Behold, how good and how pleasant it is
when brothers also dwell together in unity . . .
From there God commanded the blessing
of everlasting life.

— CHAPTER 29 —

Fear

Fear is the greatest equalizer there is. Where wealth, size, or strength may give one a sense of superiority, fear can immediately level the playing field.

Go to any doctor's office or emergency room and watch the reaction of big, muscular, powerful Schwarzenegger-type men. Watch as the doctor approaches with a needle!

Women, the so called "fairer sex," the "weaker sex," are quick to point out how if the big brave men had to deliver the babies, our race would have ended long ago. Men fear pain!

There are few things more frustrating than dealing with people who are phobic. Otherwise developed and talented people have uncontrollable and irrational fears that take over their lives. It can be so debilitating that they cannot leave their houses or function in any way in society.

Psychotherapist Sheldon Kopp says that one of the greatest challenges of his profession is to help people overcome their fears. Only then can a person realize his or her true potential.

Kopp cherishes a story from his father's childhood that illustrates how unreasonable fears overwhelm us at times.

Kopp's father grew up in desperate poverty in the heart of New York City. As a boy, he would often hang around the local shipyards and throw stones at the coal barges that sailed in and out of the harbor. To drive him away, the men on the barges threw pieces of coal at the boy. By collecting these pieces of coal, the little boy helped his family to heat their home in the winter.

One day, the boy's mother gave him a nickel and sent him to the day-old bakery to buy some bread. The bread only cost two cents, so she expected her son to bring back exactly three cents in change.

It was a cold winter day, and the boy was clad only in a threadbare sweater with six pockets. He walked the long route to the bakery and bought his two cents' worth of bread, then made the long trip back in the cold.

As the boy neared home, he began to worry about those three pennies in change. If he lost even one penny, he would be in for a beating.

So he reached into one of the six pockets and fished around for the change. It wasn't there. Frantically, he reached into four of his other pockets. No pennies anywhere. He had only one other pocket to check. But he couldn't bring himself to reach into that last pocket. He just couldn't confront his awful fear that he had lost the three pennies.

So Sheldon Kopp's father sat out on his front porch for hours in the cold. If he looked in his one remaining pocket, he feared discovering that the money was gone. If he went inside, he feared facing his parents and their anger.

So he sat outside in the numbing cold, paralyzed by competing fears he just couldn't bring himself to face.[1]

Try to make a list of all the things you are afraid of. It will in all likelihood be quite long, and as you think, it will continue to grow.

When we're young, we're scared of the dark and of the "boogey man." When our parents argue, we are scared they may leave us, or each other. We're scared of the school bully, of the lightning, of the barking dog, and the deep water. We hear of death and we fear losing a parent, we see fire and we're scared of being burned.

---

1. Kopp, Sheldon, *Raise Your Right Hand Against Fear, Extend the Other in Compassion* (New York: Ballantine Books, 1988, 75-76. *Dynamic Preaching,* July 1998, p.39-40.

This primitive list grows dramatically as life becomes more complex.

In school we fear bad grades on tests, or failing the year. We fear parental disapproval almost as much as we are terrified of social rejection.

Over the adult years, what don't we fear? We fear never meeting a love partner, and then we fear we've met the wrong one. We fear we will be unemployed, and then we fear we will be stuck in an unsatisfying job for life. We fear being poor, and if we have money we fear losing it. We fear the IRS and its terrible tool, the audit. We fear the test results at the doctor's study, and we fear being called into the boss's office.

The list is endless—and then we have children.

Now the fears begin all over again.

We now carry our own fears as well as our projected fears for them. They say that as you get older, you need and indeed get less sleep. If I can judge from my parents, you sleep so poorly because at that stage you have grandchildren and can worry about three generations all at once.

We don't want to fear—we just can't help it. We fight every day to overcome it, yet just as we're about to conquer the fear, something is thrown in our face to unsettle us again.

I have a mild fear of flying. It's more of the white-knuckle type than a debilitating phobia. After a couple of uneventful trips I feel less anxiety as we are about to take off. Then I read of a plane crash, and on the next two outings I am back to the clenched-fist, deep-breath takeoffs.

In spite of our prosperity, in spite of modern science and advanced knowledge in so many fields, we are apprehensive. That's what surveys show. We view the future with concern and even alarm.

Someone asked, "Will my life have a storybook ending?"

Someone else answered, "Are you familiar with Stephen King?" [2]

So how do we deal with these fears?

There are the short-term answers.

We can escape. We can drink or take drugs and escape the

---

2. *Dynamic Preaching,* July 1998, p. 36.

pain and paralysis of fear. For as long as we are drunk or high, we can sing and be blissful. We can block out the anxieties that come with life, and we can retreat to a painless world. There, we can forget our problems and escape the worry. Unfortunately, at some point you sober up. The high will end, and when you come down, the problem will still be there. The fear remains as great, or is perhaps greater since the last "trip" away.

Another way is to try to solve the specific problem—to make the symptoms go away without dealing with the underlying problem.

Bruce Larson tells about a man who had terrible hallucinations that plagued him for a number of years.

"I believed that there were wild, hideous animals hiding under my bed," the man told one of his friends. "Every night when the lights went out, they would come out, prowl all around the room, and scare the stew out of me. But my brother finally solved my problem."

"Oh, is he a psychiatrist?" asked his friend.

"No," said the man, "he's a carpenter. He sawed the legs off my bed."[3]

The real solution comes in the comfort of knowing that you will somehow be all right. Problems are not so overwhelming that there is no hope for the future. You need to believe that you will overcome and succeed, and then you will.

Setbacks will be seen for what they are: short-term problems that will pass, not insurmountable obstacles. Even failure will be seen as part of the process and not as a reason to become inactive. This message, though, needs to come from an authoritative source.

When I was a youngster, I had my share of worries. For years, I could not sleep without listening to talk radio. I needed something to divert my mind from day-to-day issues; otherwise, I would stay awake worrying all night.

The night before a test was particularly challenging, notwithstanding hours of review and preparation. In those years, it was often enough for a parent, sensing my restlessness, to come into my bedroom and tell me that all would be fine. The

---

3. *Dynamic preaching*, Oct 1998, p. 5.

power that came with being the parent, the aura of authority and experience, was often enough to get me through the immediate crisis.

As we get older and the fallibility of our parents becomes clearer, we need a greater authority to tell us that it will be okay. We need to have faith in something or someone, to give us the inner strength to overcome our fears. We need a faith in a "superparent," and how fortunate for believers that we have one we call God.

This is the message of Psalm 91. It is all about not having to fear, because we will be protected by God.

This psalm is different from most of the other psalms, because it has two voices that speak or even preach to an unknown third party, who is the recipient of this message. Here the psalmist is not dealing with his own problem or crisis. He is not giving thanks for something that happened to him. He is reaching out to someone in need, someone in great fear, and he is giving him the assurance that it will all work out for the best. Then, most amazingly, but in line with the psychology of support that I mention above, he brings in God Himself to speak. God assures the listener that it will be all right. He need not fear, for God is with him.

Read the beginning verses of this psalm as if you are the one with all the fears and the psalmist is talking to you. Then listen as God takes over toward the end.

Oh you who dwell in the shelter of the Most High
and abide in the protection of Shaddai,
I say of the Lord, my refuge and stronghold,
MY God in whom I trust,
that He will save you from the fowler's trap,
from the destructive plague.
He will cover you with His pinions;
you will find refuge under His wings;
His fidelity is an encircling shield.
You need not fear the terror by night,
or the arrow that flies by day;
the plague that stalks in the darkness,
or the scourge that ravages at noon.

A thousand may fall at your left side,
ten thousand at your right,
but it shall not reach you.
You will see it with your eyes,
you will witness the punishment of the wicked.
Because you took the Lord—my refuge
the Most High—as your haven,
no harm will befall you,
no disease touch your tent.
For He will order His angels
to guard you wherever you go.
They will carry you in their hands
lest you hurt your foot on a stone.
You will tread on cubs and vipers;
you will trample lions and asps. (vs. 1-13)

Now we have the switch in voice from the psalmist to God.

Because he is devoted to Me, I will deliver him;
I will keep him safe, for he knows My name.
When he calls on Me, I will answer him;
I will be with him in distress;
I will rescue him and make him honored;
I will let him live to a ripe old age
and show him My salvation. (vs. 14-16)

God's is the voice of our final comfort, but only if you truly believe it. The following short story explains how we have to hear and understand His voice.

During a terrible thunderstorm, a man ran up to his five-year-old daughter's room, fearing that she would be petrified.

He got up to her room and saw his daughter standing on the windowsill, leaning spread-eagle against the glass of the windowpanes, with lightning and thunder flashing and roaring outside.

The father said, "Jennifer, what are you doing?"

The little girl replied, filled with delight, "Dad, I think God's trying to take my picture."[4]

You have to know that God cares about you. Then these words can truly alleviate anxiety and fear.

say of the Lord, my refuge and stronghold,
MY God in whom I trust,
that He will save you.

Postscript:
The psalm raises one other fascinating issue. It talks about the angels:

For He will order His angels
to guard you wherever you go.
They will carry you in their hands
lest you hurt your foot on a stone.

Who and what are they? We'll try to find out in the next chapter.

A warning to the reader. If you have trouble with the concept that God spoke and thus the world came into being, you'll definitely want to skip the next chapter.

---

4. By Elliot Gertel, *The American Rabbi,* Dec. 1994, page 30.

— CHAPTER 30 —

Angels or Men?

Jimmy Stewart was one of my favorite actors. His characters had such strength and dignity. Much of this was the result of him being raised by loving and honorable parents.

Jimmy Stewart wrote of how when he was leaving to fight in World War II, his father sent him a letter with wise and loving advice. His dad, Alex Stewart, wrote, "My dear Jim Boy, soon after you read this letter, you will be on your way to the worst sort of danger. I am banking on the enclosed copy of the 91st Psalm. The thing that takes the place of fear and worry is the promise of these words. . . . I can say no more . . . I love you more than I can tell you. Dad."

Part of that psalm reads,

For He will order His angels
to guard you wherever you go.
They will carry you in their hands
lest you hurt your foot on a stone. (vs. 11, 12)

The reference to angels in Psalm 91 was no fluke or exception. It was no passing metaphor or allegory. It is very much a part of the reality of the Bible's understanding of how the universe functions. When God created the world in Genesis, He

169

said, "Let us make mankind in our Image" (1:26). Whom was he talking to? Tradition answers, with angels.

When Adam and Eve were expelled from the Garden of Eden, it says (3:24), "So He drove out the man; and He placed the Cherubim (angels) at the east of the Garden of Eden."

When Abraham was about to execute his son Isaac, it says (22:11) "And an angel of the Lord called to him out of Heaven, and said, 'Abraham, Abraham.'"

When Hagar was dying in the desert, having been banished with her son Ishmael by Abraham, the Bible says (21:17), "And God heard the voice of the lad; and the angel of God called out to Hagar out of heaven, and said to her . . ."

When Jacob flees his homeland after tricking his father into giving him the birthright, he makes camp at nightfall and goes to sleep. The Bible then says (28:12), "And he dreamed, and behold a ladder set up on the earth, and the top of it reached to heaven, and behold the angels of God ascending and descending on it."

When Isaiah is called to prophecy, he sees God surrounded by angels called Seraphim (Isaiah 6:2). "Seraphim stood above Him: each one had six wings; with two he covered his face, and with two he covered his feet, and with two He did fly . . ."

It is no wonder, then, that angels are a very real part of the psalmist's understanding of how the world works. This he tells us very clearly in Psalm 103.

The Lord has established His throne in heaven,
and his sovereign rule is over all.
Bless the Lord, O His angels,
mighty creatures who do His bidding,
ever obedient to His bidding;
bless the Lord, all His hosts,
His servants who do His will;
bless the Lord, all His works,
through the length and breadth of His realm;
bless the Lord, O my soul. (vs. 19-22)

The rabbinic world that formed the Judaism of today accepted the existence of angels as a given part of their universe.

About eighteen centuries ago, the colleagues of the great sage Rabbi Judah stood around him when he was gravely ill. They prayed ceaselessly for his recovery. But every person has a destined life span beyond which even love and prayer, doctors, nurses, and medication fail. And so, Rabbi Judah returned to his Maker.

An attending rabbi was delegated to convey the news to those anxiously waiting to hear. This is how he conveyed his message. He said, "The angels in heaven and the angels on earth fought for the holy ark (the soul of Judah). The angels in heaven won."

Certainly the existence of angels has always been a part of the theology of Christianity. It is difficult to view any of the great medieval or later Renaissance paintings without finding the strong presence of angels.

It is only in the modern, rational world that people of all faiths have tended to suppress the belief in angels. The verses are explained away as symbolic or metaphoric language. Customs or practices that existed specifically because of angels were now seen to be quaint folk practices, or else something for the children that the parents smiled or winked at.

When a Jew returns from synagogue on Friday night, he sings a song at the Sabbath table in which he welcomes the ministering angels who escorted him home safely. That's what the words say, but few hear it that way. Yet the practice was originated by people who very literally believed in personal guardian angels, and this song was a very real welcome and thank-you to them.

The Kabbalistic or mystical view of Judaism absolutely affirms the existence of angels. The belief—and this was certainly held by the psalmist—was that God created a physical world that we can see understand and experience. He also created a spiritual world. We cannot detect this world by physical means. It is a matter of belief and traditional teachings. It is in the spiritual world that two types of entities exist.

One is what we call the soul, which will eventually enter the physical world in a body. The other entity is a spiritual body that will forever be limited to the spiritual world. These are called angels.

For whatever reason, God chose to relate to the physical

world through the agency of angels. Every physical entity and process is under the charge of some type of angel. Rabbinic literature expresses it as follows: "There is no blade of grass down below that does not have an angel on high that strikes it and tells it to grow" (Genesis Rabbah 10:16).

God has chosen that His decrees should be translated into action in this world through angels. Each is appointed in its own area of influence. Do we really understand what this means, and why? I would argue no, and it doesn't really matter. It's like the following story.

A woman moved to a cave high in the mountains to study with a guru. She wanted to learn everything there was to know. The guru supplied her with stacks of books and left her alone so she could study.

Every morning, the guru returned to the cave to monitor the woman's progress. In his hand he carried a heavy wooden cane. Each morning, he asked her the same question: "Have you learned everything there is to know yet?"

Her answer was always the same. "No," she said, "I haven't." The guru would then strike her over the head with his cane. This pattern repeated itself for months.

One day, the guru entered the cave, asked the same question, heard the same answer, and raised his cane to hit her in the same way.

Suddenly, the woman grabbed the cane from his hand, stopping the guru's assault in midair. Relieved to end the daily beating but fearing reprisal, the woman looked up at the guru.

To her surprise, the guru smiled. "Congratulations," he said. "You have graduated. You now know everything you need to know."

"What do you mean?" the woman asked.

The guru replied, "You have learned that you will never comprehend everything there is to know. And now you have learned how to stop the pain."[1]

We don't really have to know how it works and why God created these angels. There are things that exist in the world that I cannot comprehend. Perhaps others with greater knowledge, piety, insight, or holiness can penetrate the secrets of God's universe. For me, it is enough to function within the world of what is revealed and from which I can learn. To me, the lesson ultimately to be learned from the angels is not about them, but about me as a human being.

We mistakenly believe that because angels are spiritual and have no bodies, they are superior parts of God's creation.

There is a story told about a new building that was being planned for the Vatican. The architect submitted the drawings to the Pope for review. They were returned with a simple comment: "*Non summus angeli*—We are not angels."

The architect couldn't figure out what the Pope meant until someone pointed out that the plans did not include bathrooms.[2]

Angels are not superior. In fact, the opposite is true. This, to me, is the profound teaching of angels. In God's creation, angels can never change. They can never sin, because they have no freedom of choice; but they can never rise or grow, either. They can never be limited or be tempted by the flesh; but they can never experience the delight of a good meal. They can never use that as an opportunity to praise their creator for the magnificence of His world. They can never commit adultery or debase their bodies; but they will never experience the ecstasy of sexual union between a husband and wife. This union is the very model that teaches us how to achieve union with our God.

I leave to God His reasons for the angels. I thank Him for whatever benefit I may derive from them. Mostly, I am appreciative of the lesson that angels teach me every day.

I am the pinnacle of God's creation. I have powers more awesome than the angels themselves. I can change and be better. I can improve and seek daily to come closer to My maker.

Bless the Lord, all His hosts,
His servants who do His will;
bless the Lord, all His works,
through the length and breadth of His realm;
bless the Lord, O my soul.

---

1. "Indiana, Let Go," by David Meyer, in the *American Rabbi*, Vol. 23, No. 5.
2. Geoffrey Haber, *American Rabbi*, July 1995, p.6.

— CHAPTER 31 —

Anger–The Debilitating Emotion

One of the great joys of reading psalms is that you constantly discover something new. You may have read a psalm a hundred times before, but on the hundred and first time, you see for the first time something that has always been there.

In chapters 7 and 8, I have already shown how different lines of Psalm 145 have related to different life experiences of mine. Imagine the shock and subsequent joy when years later, while studying the psalm, I discovered a whole new message based not on word but on structure.

I was reading and analyzing the psalm when I noticed that one verse didn't fit. It actually was radically different than anything that preceded it.

The psalm is a praise or ode to God It speaks first of the psalmist's constant praise of God.

> *I will extol You, my God and king*
> *and bless Your name forever and ever.*
> *Every day I will bless You*
> *and praise Your name forever and ever.*
> *Great is the Lord and much acclaimed;*
> *His greatness cannot be fathomed.*
> *One generation shall laud Your works to another*

and declare Your mighty acts.
The glorious majesty of Your splendor
and Your wondrous acts will I recite.
Men shall talk of the might of Your awesome deeds,
and I will recount your greatness.
They shall celebrate Your abundant goodness
and sing joyously of Your greatness. (vs. 1-7)

Then it changes to a description of the wondrous deeds of God. They are unqualified. They flow from the goodness of God, unearned but available to all.

The Lord is gracious and compassionate,
slow to anger and abounding in kindness.
The Lord is good to all,
and His mercy is upon all His works. (vs. 8-9)

Your kingship is an eternal kingship;
Your dominion is for all generations.
The Lord supports all who stumble
and makes all who are bent stand straight.
The eyes of all look to You expectantly,
and You give them their food when it is due.
You give it openhandedly,
feeding every creature to its heart's content.
The Lord is beneficent in all His ways
and faithful in all His works. (vs. 13-17)

And then, suddenly, it changes. The tone and the substance do a radical about-face. Now there is a qualifier. There is a condition before which God will help out.

The Lord is near to all who call Him,
to all who call Him with sincerity.
He fulfills the wishes of those who fear Him;
He hears their cry and delivers them.
The Lord watches over all who love Him,
but all the wicked He will destroy. (vs. 18-20)

His goodness, His grace is dependent on your behavior. It is limited and conditional. It is not the God of the first part of the psalm. Then it turns again:

My mouth shall utter the praise of the Lord,
and all the creatures shall bless His holy name forever and ever.
(vs. 21)

What happened here? How could God change so much? Or did He? I believe that what we have here is not a chronicle of a changing God, but rather a view of a maturing and therefore changing human being.

The first and longest part of the psalm is reflective of our youth and the first half of adulthood. There are natural developmental stages and processes that we need to achieve.

Susan Strasberg once said to a therapist, "It hurt so much to grow up—no wonder people don't want to do it."

And the therapist said, "If you had done it when you were supposed to, it wouldn't have hurt so much."

In our youth we are idealistic, optimistic, enthusiastic, and often naive. It is normal for us to be full of vigor and love for God. The whole world lies ahead of us. Our future is uncharted and we are told that we "can achieve anything we set our hearts to achieve."

It is part of the mythology of youth that if we study hard enough and work hard enough, then the rewards of a good life will be waiting at our feet. Much of the book of Genesis exists to teach that in spite of the dominance of the first-born in the ancient world, it doesn't have to be that way.

Abraham was not the eldest, but he believed in God and became the chosen one. Isaac was younger than Ishmael. Jacob was younger than Esau, and Joseph younger than many of his brothers. Yet leadership went to the one who earned it, not the one who was born into it.

It was easy and natural for the young psalmist to praise God for all that He does.

The Lord is good to all,
and His mercy is upon all His works.

But then real life takes over.

You work very hard for twenty years for your company, only to be laid off in downsizing. You see someone infinitely less talented than you achieve great material success, and you are still struggling to find your way. Your marriage, begun with such warmth and love, is now a cold empty shell of mutual convenience. Your children grow away from you and your plans for them. You change. You become angry. You no longer see the world and God through such rosy and optimistic eyes.

God is there, all right, but not for everyone. There must be a reason why some receive and some do not. It must, in fact, be conditional.

The Lord is near to all who call Him,
to all who call Him with sincerity.
He fulfills the wishes of those who fear Him;
He hears their cry and delivers them.
The Lord watches over all who love Him,
but all the wicked He will destroy.

The psalmist is angry and disappointed and he wants punishment. He's not in a mood to be forgiving, accepting, or compassionate. Nor does he want God to be!

In his autobiography, Simon Wiesenthal tells a story about himself.

After the war, a man living near him in one of the displaced persons camps borrowed the equivalent of ten dollars from him. He assured him that he had a package coming from a relative any day and would definitely pay him back the next week. At week's end, he had an excuse for not paying, and the next week, he had an even better one. So it went on for almost a year.

Finally one day, the man came up to him with cash in hand and said, "My visa has just come through. I'm leaving for Canada tomorrow. Here's the money I owe you."

Wiesenthal waved him away and said, "No, keep it. For ten dollars, it's not worth changing my opinion of you."[1]

But the psalm doesn't end that way. There is another stage

---

1. *The American Rabbi,* Fall 1997.

left in life. After the disappointment seen in midlife, we acquire if lucky, a certain wisdom of old age. We gain perspective. Life is not so black-and-white. We learn to appreciate the good and tolerate the bad in life. Our expectations are more realistic, and our experiences have enabled us to grow. We learn to give up anger as a negative and ultimately self-draining emotion.

The Midrash (Jewish lore) teaches, "When a kettle boils, it spills hot water down its side."

If we boil over with anger, we scald ourselves.

When a rattlesnake becomes angry, it often winds up biting itself.

Anger never improves a situation. It can't clean up the past, it can only muddy the future. To learn that lesson is to arrive at the end of this psalm.

It happened once to a great Hasidic master, the Apter Rav, Abraham Joshua Heschel.

One day Rabbi Heschel received a visitor, a woman known only too well for her conduct. Whatever people of loose and malicious tongues say about such a woman, they said about her.

She approached Rabbi Heschel as he sat among his disciples.

"Rabbi," she began, "I need your help, your intervention for me in heaven. I want to repent. I want to change my ways. Please help me."

The Apter Rav, known for his gentle and gracious ways, responded with anger. "You dare come to me? Shameless woman, you have the temerity to appear before me? Don't you realize that I have eyes to see, and that my eyes see into your innermost soul?" To prove his words, the Apter Rav proceeded to reveal certain things she had done.

The woman blushed and then answered gently and sadly, "I don't understand you, Rabbi. Why must you reveal in public what God Himself prefers to keep secret?"

Later, the Apter Rav reflected on what he had done and was troubled to his core. He said to his disciples who had witnessed his explosion, "This encounter has humbled me; it will remain a turning point in my life. It made me see that I was on the wrong path, for I chose judgment over compassion. Our task is not to judge other human beings, not to condemn others, but to understand them."[2]

In modern times, this lesson was learned yet again but with a different twist In a letter to Ann Landers, a woman writes how she learned to deal effectively with her anger and in the process bring everyone a little closer in joy and harmony:

> Last year, I learned of a good way to reduce stress. After an upsetting confrontation with a rude sales clerk, I got in my car to go to the bank. I was so angry I couldn't see straight.
>
> On my way, I passed a donut shop and impulsively stopped. I bought a dozen doughnuts, took them to the bank, and gave them to the tellers for their coffee break. My anger was immediately dispelled, and I felt good the rest of the day.
>
> That was the first time I performed a random act of kindness and have since made it a habit. The results are magical.[3]

The psalmist grew up. He let go of his anger and judgmental behavior. He achieved a peace for himself and a universal outlook for all mankind.

My mouth shall utter the praise of the Lord,
and all the creatures shall bless His holy name forever and ever.

---

2. *The American Rabbi*, April 1994, page 49.
3. Ann Landers, 1994.

— CHAPTER 32 —

You, Too, Can Get There

During the sabbatical year in which I've been writing this book I've had the opportunity to live in different parts of the world. In the fall I lived in Melbourne, Australia, and in the spring I resided in Jerusalem. There, I was able to celebrate the freedom festival of Passover.

During the same week, I observed the Moslems celebrate a festival, and I watched as Christian pilgrims from all over the world came to celebrate Easter. There was great holiness in the air.

One could feel the potential for unity of the three sibling religions, if they could only pause to realize how much they shared under the divinity of the same God.

A short time later, Israel observed a memorial day for its fallen soldiers who died in defense of the country. The day was somber. It included many memorial services, and at 11:00 A.M., a siren blasted and the country stood still for two minutes of silence.

On every street, even every highway, vehicles halted on the spot. Drivers emerged from their cars and stood at attention in somber memory.

That evening, synagogues concluded the day with memorial

prayers. Suddenly the darkness lifted and everyone emerged into the streets to party.

They began twenty-four hours of great fun and jubilation as they observed the fifty-first anniversary of the State of Israel.

During those two days, one psalm was quoted over and over again. It was Psalm 137. This psalm was written by Jews who survived the destruction of the first state of Israel by the Babylonians in the year 586 B.C.E.

They were forced into exile in Babylonia (Iraq), where they longed for their lost country, and wrote:

By the rivers of Babylon,
there we sat,
sat and wept,
as we thought of Zion.
There on the poplars
we hung up our lyres,
for our captors asked us there for songs,
our tormentors for amusement:
"Sing us one of the songs of Zion."
How can we sing a song of the Lord
on alien soil?
If I forget thee, O Jerusalem
let my right hand wither,
let my tongue stick to my palate
if I cease to think of you,
if I do not keep Jerusalem in memory
even at my happiest hour. (vs. 1-5)

A few months later, something very special happened. I came across a story that reminded me yet again of the awesome power of Psalms and its universal message.

Gilbert Beers, former editor of *Christianity Today*, tells a story that has helped shape his family for many generations. Beer's eighth great-grandmother lived in a small settlement called Paltz, New York.

Back in 1663, Minnisink Indians attacked Paltz and kidnaped a group of women and children from the settlement.

Gilbert's eighth great-grandmother, Catherine duBois, and her little daughter, Sara, were two of those taken captive.

After spending ten weeks hidden away in the Catskill Mountains, the Minnisinks were sure they had outwaited any search party. To celebrate their conquest, the Indians decided to burn Catherine and Sara on a special pyre. The pyre was built, and Catherine was tied up, and she and her daughter were placed on it. Any normal person probably would have faced such a death with screams, curses, and hopelessness. Not Catherine duBois. She began to sing a Huguenot hymn taken from Psalm 137:

> *For our captors asked us there for songs,*
> *our tormentors for amusement:*
> *"Sing us one of the songs of Zion."*

When she finished, something extraordinary happened. The Minnisinks did not light the pyre. Instead, they asked Catherine to sing another song. And then another. And while she was singing, the search party from Paltz appeared and rescued her whole party.

Catherine duBois drew upon her faith in the greatest time of crisis she probably ever faced. Little did anyone dream that her example would inspire eight generations to cling to their Christian faith.

Gilbet Beers says, "The God I prayed to this morning is the same God Catherine sang to eight generations ago, the same God who will listen to one of my faithful decendents eight generations from now. The God who heard Catherine's Huguenot hymn 324 years ago hears my prayer of thanksgiving today for her faithfulness." [1]

Once again I was reminded in the clearest way of my original reason for writing this book. The power of the psalms is universal. For Jews or for Christians, from modern Israel to colonial America, Psalms has the power to inspire. Sometimes it comes from the power of the message. Sometimes it is the tool for the reinforcing of faith.

In Catherine's time of trouble, it was the source of her comfort

---

1. *Dynamic Preaching*, July 1998, p. 47.

and faith. In my time of personal sadness, it was a source of strength and encouragement that enabled me to get on with my life.

I hope the chapters and stories in this book will send readers of all backgrounds to this great gift of inspiration and spiritual healing.

In distress I called on the Lord;
the Lord answered me and brought me relief.
The Lord is on my side;
I have no fear. . . (Ps. 118, vs. 5, 6)

Index of Psalms

About the Author

RABBI PAUL PLOTKIN is the Senior Rabbi of Temple Beth Am in Margate, Florida. His many professional affiliations include the presidency (1988–90) of the Rabbinical Assembly of America, Southeast Region, and membership in the Committee on Jewish Law and Standards of the International Rabbinical Assembly. His travels have taken him to Israel, Australia, Europe, Jerusalem, and throughout the Orient.

Rabbi Plotkin produced and hosted a weekly television show, *The Temple Israel Hour.* He lectures on death and dying, Jewish myth, magic and superstition, Kashruth and Kabbalah.